Miniature Orchids

TO GROW AND SHOW

W·W·NORTON & COMPANY·NEW YORK·LONDON

Miniature Orchids

TO GROW AND SHOW

Jack Kramer

WITH ROY L. CRAFTON

DRAWINGS BY CAROL CARLSON
& ANDREW ROY ADDKISON

FIRST EDITION

The text of this book is composed in VIP Primer, with display type set in Egmont
Medium. Manufacturing by Vail-Ballou Press, Inc. Book design by Antonina Krass.

Library of Congress Cataloging in Publication Data
Kramer, Jack, 1927–
Miniature orchids to grow and show.
Includes index.
1. Miniature orchids.   2. Orchid culture.
I. Crafton, Roy L.   II. Title.
SB409.K7157   635.9'3415   82–6352
AACR2

W. W. Norton & Company, Inc. 500 Fifth Avenue, New York, N.Y. 10110
W. W. Norton & Company Ltd. 37 Great Russell Street, London WC1B 3NU

1 2 3 4 5 6 7 8 9 0

ISBN 0-393-01632-3

Contents

Contents · 9

Contents · 10

SIX

Other Miniature Orchids · 181

Miniature Orchids

TO GROW AND SHOW

ONE

The World of Miniature Orchids

There is something infinitely charming about the diminutive—think of miniature dolls and houses, for example. The same holds true for the world of flowers. Among large plants, there are true miniature plants in many groups: begonias, cacti, gesneriads, to name a few. The one producing perhaps the largest number of miniatures is also the most advanced group of plants in the world: the orchids. Small flowers on tiny plants by any genus are irresistible, but the delight afforded by miniature orchids is special. Fortunately, even the most cramped apartment can accommodate a few miniature orchids.

The small orchids do well on windowsills, where you can grow a dozen or more plants in a small space; in handsome terrariums as accent pieces throughout the home; and in bell jars or other decorative glass containers that highlight the beauty of the blooms. Orchids are extremely decorative and will elicit comments and admiration from guests (see chapter 3).

Many orchids grow in trees, festooning branches with color; this photo shows a collector in Ecuador. (PHOTO COURTESY PAUL HUTCHINSON)

Orchids also grow on rocks; here we see a splendid large Oncidium specimen in Chile. (PHOTO COURTESY PAUL HUTCHINSON)

You can also grow miniature orchids on pieces of cork bark or tree fern slabs. This is the natural way of growing them, and plants do amazingly well when cultivated in this manner, because they receive the plentiful amount of air they need to thrive. You can even fashion miniature orchid trees from small branches. In later chapters we will explore the various ways of growing and enjoying the miniatures.

ORCHIDS AND WHERE THEY COME FROM

Success with any plant—miniature or otherwise—depends on knowing something about the plant, where it comes from (this gives you a clue to cultural requirements), and how it grows (this gives you an idea of how you can grow the plant). So let us spend some time with the diminutive giants of the orchid clan.

Like their cousins the standard-size plants, miniature orchids come from many parts of the world, but most originate on the west coast of South America, Central America, and, in great number, New Guinea. Areas of Asia, Africa, and Borneo also have vast orchid regions. And there are some locations, like the Grand Cayman Islands south of Cuba, where only one species thrives, growing there and nowhere else.

Growing conditions vary widely. The Pleione orchid, a true small plant, often breaks through snow to bloom, and several small Angraecums are hardly visible in steaming East African jungles. Although most orchids dwell in treetops at elevations of about 5,500 feet in tropical rain forests, there are species that are terrestrial and thrive at sea level, and others, like the miniatures *Telipogon angustifolia* and *Restrepia elegans,* that enjoy life on rocks or tree branches at 7,000 to 9,000 feet.

Generally, the orchids that grow on the forest floor receive constant heat (70°F. night and day). However, for every 1,000 feet, the temperature drops about 5 degrees. Because most orchid species grow at elevations between 2,000 and 6,000 feet, with temperatures between 50° and 90°F., they are quite accustomed to cool evenings. The west coast of South America—Chile, Peru, Ecuador, and Colombia—is rich in orchids; hundreds flourish here. The terrain is very mountainous, and at 6,000 feet the temperature is 48°F. at night.

In nature, both arboreal or terrestrial orchids generally inhabit areas of moderate, not high, temperatures and grow where there is good air circulation. It is wise to remember this when selecting places for orchids in your home or greenhouse.

How They Grow

Some orchids grow in the ground like ordinary plants, others hug rocks for survival, and a great many species cling to tree branches in rain forests as epiphytes—"epi" meaning on and "phyte" meaning plant. The orchids do not derive any nourishment from their hosts; they grow where they can find a foothold. If a tree is not handy, orchids wll survive on a fallen log, a roof, and even on other plants. Generally, epiphytes have an extensive root network that catches dead leaves, insects, twigs, and dust. Rain eventually dissolves this miscellaneous matter that furnishes nutrients to the plants.

Orchid flowers, although they may not all look alike, always share three characteristics: (1) three sepals, (2) three petals, and (3) a column. The sepals are usually extended and the petals usually modified into a lip formation. The column is a fleshy projection that contains the reproductive organs. This unique modification exists only in the orchid family. No matter how large or small an orchid flower is, these structural elements always are present.

Orchids are generally arboreal or epiphytic (air plants); some are terrestrials and grow in the ground like other plants, and many grow on rocks—how they grow depends on climatic conditions.

Orchids grow either in a monopodial or sympodial manner. If monopodial, this simply means that they grow or creep in one direction continuously. A single stem lengthens season after season. Sympodial orchids, on the other hand, grow horizontally. Year after year lateral shoots climb upwards. Most sympodial orchids have elongated branches or pseudobulbs—food storage organs for water and nutrients.

FLOWERS

Among the *Orchidaceae* (the orchid family), the range of size, color, and form of blossoms is truely dramatic. Miniatures of some Bulbophyllum and Stelis species have tiny blossoms, many only $1/32$ inch in diameter. The flowers may be single or in groups, or there may be as many as fifty blossoms to each stalk, as occurs in the Candlestick orchid, *Stenoglottis longifolia*. Except for true black, orchid flowers are produced in all colors and combinations of colors and hues, with bright yellow, vivid red, and pure white predominating.

Many orchids are heavily scented; even one such plant perfumes an entire room. *Brassavola nodosa,* only 12 inches tall, has a lily-of-the-valley scent. Not all are so pleasant. *Bulbophyllum careyanum,* for

TYPES OF FLOWERS

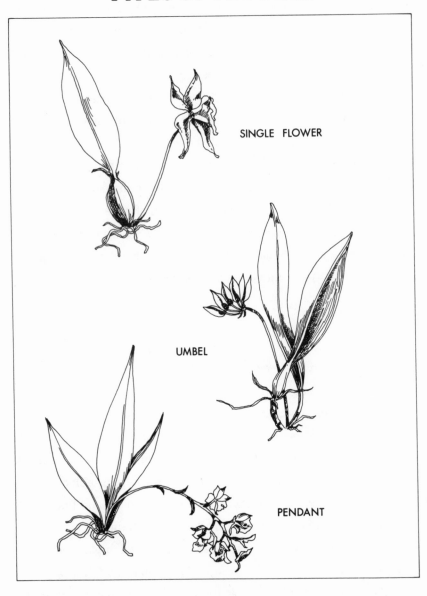

SINGLE FLOWER

UMBEL

PENDANT

The beauty of the miniature blossom can be seen in this close-up of *Stelis ruprichtiana;* the flowers are ¼ inch across. (PHOTO BY ROY CRAFTON)

Some small Oncidiums (left) and a Phalaenopsis make a handsome silhouette against a window. (PHOTO BY ROY CRAFTON)

instance, can drive you from your home, so it is best to avoid this orchid.

Orchid flowers are great mimics. Some Masdevallias look like small bright kites, and many Cirrhopetalums resemble birds in flight; others, like Bulbophyllums, mimic insects—nature's way to attract insect pollenators for the plants.

NAMES AND MORE NAMES

Plant names sometimes intimidate people, but they shouldn't. To put it simply, plants are grouped in genera (singular genus), and within these groups are species that share botanical characteristics, such as number of petals and so forth. In the *Orchidaceae,* the genus might be *Cirrhopetalum* and the species, *roxburghii* (*C. roxburghii*). The species name derives either from the person who discovered it or the region where the species was found. *C. roxburghii* was found by a man named Roxburghi; *Stelis guatemalenis* grows in Guatemala.

In addition to botanical names, there are common names that have evolved for orchids over the years. The name moon orchid (*Phalaenopsis*) came into being because the blooms last longer than a moon, or a month. *Ornithocephalus* species are referred to as Bird's Head orchids, because the tiny flowers resemble nests. The flower of the Bee orchid (*Trichoceros*) looks like a bee.

In buying orchids, whenever possible ask for them by botanical name. Common names may differ from country to country.

In this book, we have followed in most cases the spelling and nomenclature of the primary horticultural reference book, *Tropica,* and *Hortus III.* On occasion we have opted for popular rather than botanical spelling, because suppliers' catalogues often carry the old or popular spellings rather than the newer botanical ones.

TWO

Buying and Selecting Plants

Years ago, miniatures were as scarce as snow in July, but today, thanks to the existence of mail-order suppliers, you can purchase hundreds of miniature plants to grow and enjoy. Most orchid nurseries are reputable, dependable, and eager to help. They are located throughout the United States, from Seattle, Washington, to Nashville, Tennessee, to Miami, Florida. An extensive list of suppliers appears at the back of this book. Write for catalogues, go through them, and make selections. Some contain photographs of the plant in flower, and we include some photographs in this book to help you make personal selections. Many mail-order suppliers charge a minimal price for the catalogue itself, but this cost generally is refundable upon purchase of a number of plants.

Do not expect to find miniature orchids at plant shops—they are unavailable. These plants are specialties, so you must go directly to the source. But this is good, because then there is no retailer who has to make a profit.

A nursery that specializes in selling orchids generally has the best selection and the widest assortment. Such a grower is always interested in your problems and willing to give advice. The grower must make you a satisfied customer if the business is to survive. In most cases the grower will tell you if the orchid is fresh from the jungle and not yet established, and he or she may even suggest that you wait to purchase the plant until it will have a better chance of growing in new surroundings. Finally, the grower will also tell you where the orchid came from, which is a vital clue to your cultivating it.

Most species orchids are not expensive—a mature plant costs from $5. to $10. However, there are more expensive plants that are difficult to find. Some, sensitive to fumigation, do not survive importation; others grow in inaccessible areas where few collectors have traveled; and in some cases the country of origin has restricted exportation to a limited number per year. Rather than pay an exorbitant price (the law of supply and demand) for such orchids, you may be better off waiting until more of them appear on the market at reasonable prices.

Many orchids are deciduous and bloom before or with new growth. Do not buy plants that already have started to grow. Inspect the base of the last pseudobulb; if there is little or no growth you will have flowers. If you see fresh growth it is best to forget these plants because generally it means it is too late for them to bloom.

A First Selection

As with all plant families, some orchid species are easier to grow than others. It is wise to start with mature plants that give you the most reward and are easy to cultivate. Once you see a few flowers, your confidence will lead to increased enthusiasm and you will be on your way to growing fine miniatures.

At first, avoid miniatures such as Pleiones and Sophronitis species, because these orchids, beautiful as they are, require special care. They are not impossible to grow indoors but you will need to have some experience with plants before cultivating the temperamental ones. Learn to crawl before you walk and all will be well in your orchid-growing venture. The essential know-how you'll need for growing the tough ones is easily learned by working with the many miniatures that are easily cultivated. Following is a typical beginner's list:

Aerides maculosum	*Gastrochilus calceolaris*
Ascocentrum miniatum	*G. dasypogon*
Brassavola nodosa	*Laelia flava*
Broughtonia sanguinea	*Leptotes bicolor*
Bulbophyllum barbigerum	*Lycaste depeii*
B. lemniscatoides	*Miltonia roezlii*
Cirrhopetalum gracillimum	*Oncidium desertorum*
Cirrhopetalum ornatissimum	*O. macropetalum*
Cirrhopetalum roxburghii	*Restrepia elegans*
Epidendrum polybulbon	*Thrixspermum formosanum*

JUNGLE PLANTS

Today, direct importation of plants from the jungles is easy and fast, and there is an element of adventure. Although you can specify which plants you want, rarely do you receive just what you ordered. Direct-import plants are shipped bare root and are subject to intense but necessary fumigation at ports of entry. These plants therefore are difficult to preserve, and you must expect some losses. However, orchids from the jungle are inexpensive (about $1.50 per plant), so incidental fatalities can be tolerated.

To buy plants directly from the source, you must obtain a permit. In the United States, a letter to the Permit Unit (Plant Quarantine Division; 209 River Street; Hoboken, NJ 07030) is all that is necessary. The Permit Unit will send you the shipping label that must be affixed to each crate of plants. Labels are issued for specific ports of entry, and you must specify a port. From Central and South America, orchids enter the United States at Miami, Florida. From western South America and the Pacific area, the plants arrive at San Francisco. From Mexico the point of entry is Brownsville, Texas. European plants arrive at Hoboken. Any collector from whom you buy your plants will request labels to accompany your shipment. Air parcel post is the best and only way to have plants sent.

As soon as the new orchids arrive, remove them from their cardboard boxes and spread them out where they can be exposed to fresh air. It is important that the lethal gas residue from fumigation be dispelled by air currents. The next day, turn the orchids so all parts of the plants have a chance to benefit from the air. After another twenty-four hours, hose the plants with water, and then let them dry in the sun for a few more days. Finally, trim or cut off dead or decaying parts, and dust all wounds with powdered charcoal.

SUNNY LOCATIONS

Not all orchids want sun. In fact, direct sun, especially in the summer, can scorch some orchids. Most orchids prefer only bright light at an eastern or western exposure. The plants fare far better in such a situation; some miniatures, like Telipogon and Stelis, will even bear their harvest of colorful flowers in a shady north window. So, obviously, selection is the key to success. In other words, select plants for the environment in which you will display them. Do not just choose plants at random. That is simply a waste of money, and, more important, you're not giving your plants the optimum growing conditions. Following is a list of plants for sunny places:

Aerides crassifolium

A. maculosum

Asocentrum pumilum

Brassavola nodosa

Comparettia falcata

Dendrobium loddigesii

D. nakaharai

Epidendrum microbulbon

Gastrochilus bellinus

Holcoglossum quasispinifolium

Laelia lundii

Pleurothallis grobyi

P. chrysantha

Restrepia elegans

SHADE AND BRIGHT LOCATIONS

When we talk about shade we are referring generally to north windows, where there is some light but where it is not as intense as, say, at an east window. In such a situation many little orchids can survive and bloom. Even if your window is obstructed by a tall building, you can still grow orchids if you make the appropriate selection. Following is a list of miniatures that tolerate a less direct exposure:

Aeranthes arachnites	*C. exul*
Angraecum compactum	*Masdevallia bella*
Bulbophyllum barbigerum	*M. caudata*
B. odoratissimum	*M. tovarensis*
Cirrhopetalum cumingii	*Phalaenopsis parishii*
C. maculosum	*Schlimia trifida*
C. watsonianum	*Stelis hymentha*
Cypripedium ang-thong	*Telipogon angustifolia*

THREE

Miniatures for All Places

Miniature orchids can be grown almost anywhere in your home or apartment—indeed, they make excellent plants for apartment dwellers whose space for plants is usually limited. Bathrooms and kitchens with at least one window or a skylight are ideal locations for plants because there is usually good humidity (about 30–40 percent) in these rooms, and windows in any room can accommodate small collections of plants. In fact, any limited space in almost any room will accommodate some small plants.

In addition to growing orchids at the windowsill, you can arrange the plants on slabs or pieces of wood and then attach the wood to a small trellis, sheet of chicken wire (available at hardware stores), or wire rack. And, of course, miniatures grow well in a terrarium or under a glass dome. Finally, you can grow your orchids in a greenhouse if you are fortunate enough to have one. There are dozens of ways to have these beautiful plants with you every day of the year.

AT WINDOWS

Having your orchids near windows gives them access to good natural light and obviously is the best arrangement for the plants. You can use glass shelves (available at hardware stores in packages with tools and other such materials), or you might want to fashion your own setups. Our drawings show various ways of arranging plants near the glass.

Another good way to display plants at windows is to use one of the various suspension-type pole units available from plant suppliers. These poles can be purchased by length; they operate with a spring compressor mechanism, so it is not necessary to drill holes into floors or ceilings. The poles come with adjustable trays, or you can make your own shelves for them as we did. (see drawing 3). The advantage of the pole system is that you can accommodate almost twenty-five plants in a limited area, and with a four-pole setup you have space for over one hundred orchids.

Another way to display plants near windows (or in a room) is to use the various types of plant stands available at plant shops. These are small spiral staircases and the steps (shelves) can accommodate several plants. The stands are portable and can be placed in various locations in the home.

The arrangement you select for your plants will depend on your specific situation and your budget.

PLACES FOR ORCHIDS

Plant shelf and 6″ galvanized pan filled with a layer of gravel

Redwood-strip tray above galvanized humidity pan

Fluorescent light fixture over table

Redwood-strip tray directly on galvanized pan

CARLSON

PLANT POLE

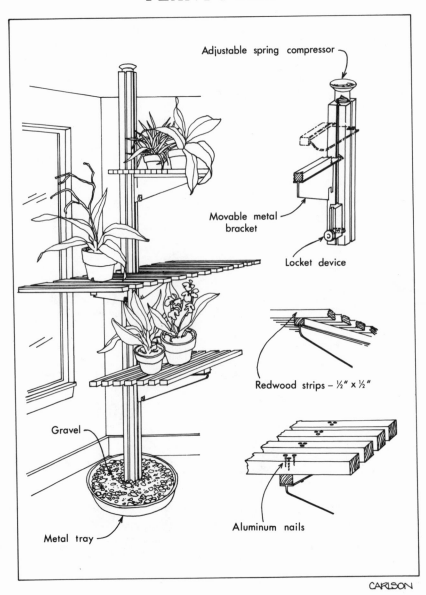

Adjustable spring compressor

Movable metal bracket

Locket device

Redwood strips – ½" x ½"

Gravel

Metal tray

Aluminum nails

CARLSON

Haraella odorata growing on a tree fern slab; small orchids do very well mounted on pieces of wood. (PHOTO BY ROY CRAFTON)

Cirrhopetalum cumingii growing on a tree fern slab; note how the small flowers form one large pattern. (PHOTO BY J. KRAMER)

Telipogon angustifolia growing on a tree branch in the wilderness.

(PHOTO COURTESY PAUL HUTCHINSON)

Ascocentrum pumilum grows on a piece of rock; note the string holding the plant to the rock. After a few months these can be cut and discarded.

(PHOTO BY ROY CRAFTON)

MOUNTING ORCHIDS ON BARK

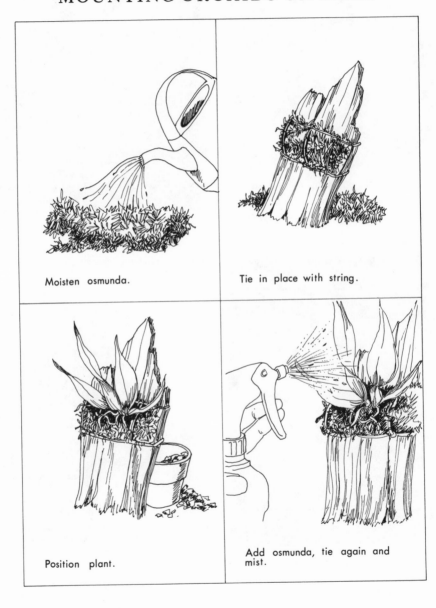

Moisten osmunda.

Tie in place with string.

Position plant.

Add osmunda, tie again and mist.

MOUNTED ORCHIDS

Many orchids grow successfully when attached to a piece of tree fern slab, a cork board, or even a small branch of a tree. The materials are available at plant suppliers. To grow orchids on these natural mountings, you must position the plants and secure the arrangement properly.

To mount an orchid on a slab or board or branch, wrap the roots in moist sphagnum or osmunda (these materials can be purchased from mail-order suppliers). Osmunda and sphagnum act as a bed for the plants and are fixed in place with string or galvanized wire (the latter available at hardware stores). Simply wrap the wire holding the plant and bedding material around the slab or board or branch. Then insert a small wire "S" hook into the mounting device and you can hang the mounted orchid on chains or wire suspended from the ceiling, as you would a basket.

To water hanging plants, remove them from the chain or wire and take them to the sink. If you have a floor that is impervious to water (tile, brick), you simply can hose down the slab or board or branch.

Orchids can also be mounted on a small trellis; these are available commercially at nurseries. Use a bed of osmunda or sphagnum (about 1 inch thick) wired to the trellis; then wire plants to the bedding material. The trellis—as described for a slab or cork board—can then be suspended from ceiling wire or chains with "S" hooks.

Wire grillwork—or oven racks, if they are not larger than, say, 12 × 20 inches—can serve in place of a wooden trellis. With a trellis

MOUNTING ORCHIDS ON RACK

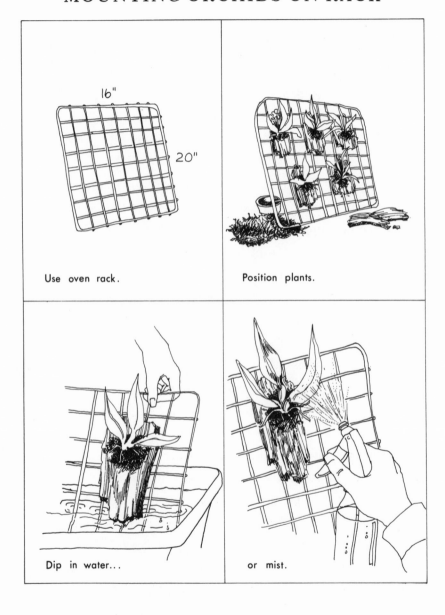

Use oven rack.

Position plants.

Dip in water...

or mist.

or oven rack you can mount as many as twenty miniatures in one area and save space.

Mounted orchids rely heavily on misting, so be prepared to spray them daily with tepid water. In hot weather, spray several times daily, and allow plants good air circulation. (See chapter 4 for more information.)

TERRARIUMS

Terrariums are glass-enclosed cases in which some miniature orchids thrive. However, in an enclosed glass case excessive condensation inside can be a problem, causing orchids to become too moist. Too much humidity can harm plants. If you are using an enclosed case, be sure to remove the lid a few hours daily so that air can circulate within; or, remove the top whenever you see excessive moisture on the glass.

There are many commercial terrariums available, in glass or plastic. Some terrariums are referred to as Wardian cases (this was a glass case used during Victorian times for plants).

Potted orchids can be placed directly into the cases., or you can first install a layer of crushed gravel and set pots upon the gravel. For a neater look, you can also use made-to-fit galvanized gravel trays at the bottom of the terrarium, or grow orchids directly in fir bark and osmunda in deep (3 to 4 inches) trays and create a miniature landscape. See which growing method you enjoy the most, or which method is easiest for you.

Again growing orchids under terrarium conditions requires spe-

Small Epidendrums make this terrarium a pleasant scene. (PHOTO BY J. KRAMER)

Views of hand-crafted terrariums. One (below) shows a terrarium planted with many miniature orchids. (PHOTO BY ROY CRAFTON)

cial care, because in a closed area air becomes stagnant. High humidity—which develops in a tightly closed case—can be a problem when coupled with cloudy days, because it provides a breeding ground for fungus disease. Eighty percent humidity over a long period can be dangerous. Keep a small hygrometer (an instrument that measures the amount of moisture in the air) in the case.

Domes

You can also grow one or several orchids under glass domes. These are available from plant suppliers and make handsome accent pieces in the home as they did in Victorian times. The glass domes, available in 8-, 10-, and 12-inch sizes, will need a base. You can use a suitable deep dish. Set the potted orchid on a 2-inch bed of gravel and cover with the glass dome. Occasionally remove dome for a few hours so plants have adequate air circulation. Growing orchids under domes requires the same care as growing them in a terrarium.

Greenhouses

Most certainly you can grow miniatures in greenhouse or window greenhouses—here, in optimum conditions, they thrive. However, do not keep the glass garden too humid. Coupled with dark days, too much moisture in the air can be damaging. Average humidity—of, say, 30 to 40 percent—will suit most orchids. In summer be sure to provide some protection from direct rays of the sun—blinds or whitewash provide shade. Above all, keep the air circulating. Orchids like a buoyant atmosphere and in stagnant conditions rarely do well.

In the greenhouse you will probably have to water orchids more than in the home—there is more light and humidity and plants dry out faster. And, obviously, keep the greenhouse clean. Faded flowers and decayed leaves or stems should be removed immediately or else disease may attack plants.

Orchids share this greenhouse with a collection of houseplants. (PHOTO COURTESY EVERLITE CO.)

FOUR

Growing Miniature Orchids

There are special tricks and things you should know about growing miniature orchids; certain conditions are different from those created for standard plants. The most important difference is that small plants generally take more time than their larger cousins to get accustomed to new conditions. In addition, proper watering of miniatures is vital to their health. Small plants, whether in pots or on slabs or bark, dry out more quickly than larger plants, so watering must be done quite regularly.

Because orchids are mainly epiphytic, they enjoy an arboreal existence with good air circulation (although, as mentioned, many do well in terrariums, too). In this chapter we cover all the aspects of growing plants indoors: watering, what to put plants in or on (containers), feeding, resting times (very vital to orchids), growing orchids under lights, and protecting plants from insects and disease.

GROWING CONDITIONS

To grow orchids (or any other plant) successfully, you must duplicate, as much as possible, their natural conditions. This does not mean that you have to convert your living room into a rain forest or build a rock garden in the kitchen. Merely consider the area you have available for the plants. If it is a window, average home temperatures are likely to prevail there: 72° to 80°F. during the day, 65° to 75° at night. Select epiphytes that will grow in these conditions. In an unheated room grow the mountainous species, such as Telipogon or Restrepia. Buy the warm-growing orchids for an east sunroom. Putting the warm growers in cool conditions will mean sure failure, as will growing the high-altitude types in heat. Selection is important, and knowing the general area a species comes from is the clue to its requirements (see chapter 5).

Information about the exact location and altitude from which an orchid comes may not always be available. Fortunately, orchids can adjust fairly well to new surroundings. Those growing high in the mountains at nighttime temperatures of 50°F. usually, when displaced, resume growth at 60°, and species that thrive naturally at 90° almost always, after a time of adjustment, respond at 80°. Thus there is some margin for error in growing orchids, more so than with other plants.

Have two areas for growing your orchids. A western exposure is somewhat warm, eastern is somewhat cool. Many orchids need coolness when resting and warmth when growing, so there is an advantage to having two areas. Some species—many Pleiones and Masdevallias—also require cold conditions: 45°F. at night. An unheated room is suitable for these beauties (note that such orchids are exceptions rather than the rule).

When situating plants, be sure there is a container under each plant or group of plants to catch the excess water that drains through the potting medium. Use 4-inch-high gravel-filled metal or plastic trays as catch basins. Orchids need bottom ventilation, so over the catch basins place 1-inch redwood strips spaced 1 inch apart, or put broken pot pieces on top of the gravel. Set the potted plants on the strips or pot pieces. Watering is made easy: excess water drains into the gravel or pot pieces and creates additional humidity.

Slabs of orchids hung at eye level are dramatic, and many species do exceptionally well when they are grown this way. To hang plants at mid-window, install screw eye-hooks into the ceiling and buy standard orchid pot hangers (available in varying lengths) from supply houses. The hanger clips onto the rim of the pot, and the curved top nests on the ceiling hook. Once again, have a container under the orchids to catch dripping water, or use clip-on saucers.

If an orchid does not do well in one location, move it to another spot. Sometimes only a few inches can make the difference between a sick orchid and a healthy one. It is fine to move blooming orchids to other parts of the house for decoration. But after they flower, return the plants to their rightful places at the windows. As mentioned, adequate ventilation is important in the growing area, so whenever possible keep nearby windows slightly open. However, do not open windows that are actually in the growing area. Where a room must be closed, run a small fan at low speed to keep the air circulating.

WATERING

If you can drink the water from your tap, so can your plants. In rare cases, where water is heavy in chlorine, you should let the water stand overnight in a bucket—to dissipate the chlorine—before watering your plants.

How you water plants is more important than when you water them. Generally, keep miniature orchids moist, except after they flower. By moist we mean uniformly wet, never soggy or dry. You can water most miniatures almost daily in hot weather, every other day in the spring and fall, and about twice a week in the winter. However, you must consider whether the plants are in pots or on slabs: with slab culture you will probably have to water your plants every other day year-round.

If the idea of watering your plants so often bothers you, or you simply do not have the time, consider growing many miniatures in one large clay container: large pots dry out more slowly than 2- or 4-inch pots. If you follow this community pot method, be sure to select plants that all require the same temperature and conditions. Our plant descriptions indicate temperature and other growing requirements.

If you are growing plants in a closed terrarium, your watering problems are lessened, because orchids in terrariums require very little water. The terrarium environment itself creates water for plants through condensation on the glass; the water runs down the glass into the enclosure. Because orchids can draw water through their leaves very efficiently, this is perhaps one of the most natural ways to grow orchids.

On sunny days, water plants more than you would on cloudy ones. It takes a combination of light and water for plants to make food, and when it is cloudy plants cannot assimilate and manufacture food from the water. With ample light and enough water, plants can produce the sugars and starches they need for growth.

HUMIDITY AND TEMPERATURE

For decades people were reluctant to grow orchids at home because of the notion that lack of humidity and/or adverse temperatures would prevent growth. In fact, though, orchids perhaps more than other popular indoor plants can, if necessary, adjust to average home temperatures and humidity. (Certainly it is better to provide maximum conditions, but this is rarely possible.) Most orchids do not need excessive sunlight; it can injure plants. Most orchids do not need high humidity (it can cause fungus disease), and most orchids can adjust to temperatures as low as 50°F. at night if necessary. So forget everything you may have read in books published some years ago: orchids do grow and grow well in average conditions. Included in the plant gallery (chapter 5) you will find humidity and temperature and light requirements for individual orchids.

COMPOSTS

There are countless numbers of growing mixtures for orchids. I do not believe that the perfect potting mix for orchids has been found;

each preparation has disadvantages and advantages.

The bark of a variety of coniferous trees, including Douglas fir and white fir, is used widely. The bark is steamed and then chopped into various grades: standard, with particles from ¼ to 1 inch; coarse, from ½- to 1-inch chunks; medium, with ¼- to 1-inch pieces; and fine, ⅛- to ¼-inch size. Fine- or medium-grade is used for miniatures; most orchids we cultivated were in fine-grade bark.

Hobby sacks of bark are sold at most nurseries and florist shops. Almost all the preparations contain sawdust fiber and dust; you should remove these particles (sift the bark through a fine-grade mesh) or it will impede water drainage.

Bark is easy to work with and inexpensive, but it does not furnish appreciable nutrients for plants, so use a standard fertilizer; 10-10-5 formula is satisfactory and should be used once a month when plants are in growth.

Years ago, osmunda was used exclusively for potting orchids. Many growers still use it today. Osmunda comes in small packages; it is the root system of two types of ferns of the genus Osmunda. This material has three advantages: (1) it deteriorates slowly and so does not have to be replaced yearly; (2) it has air spaces between its fibers, which ensures drainage; and (3) it furnishes some nutrients for plant growth. The disadvantage is that it is tough to work with and must be soaked overnight in water then cut into workable chunks.

Preparations of perlite and styrofoam pellets or gravel for orchid growing are still new. Much research is still needed before we know if these materials help produce healthy plants.

Some claims of success have been made by orchid growers who

use various kinds of tree fern fiber, called *hapu,* for growing orchids. Tree fern fiber is available in large and small pieces and in a shredded form.

CONTAINERS

Generally, standard clay pots are best for orchids. If you want a special container as an accent piece when the plant is in bloom, merely slip the clay pot into a more elaborate container.

POTTING/REPOTTING

To pot with bark, fill a pot one-third full with broken clay pieces. Scatter about ¼ inch of fresh bark into the bottom of the pot; set the plant in place, and fill in and around it with the bark, pressing down with a blunt-edged potting stick or a piece of wood. Work from the sides of the pot to the center until you have filled the pot to within ¼ inch of its rim. Most orchids require tight potting: you should be able to lift the plant by its leaves without pulling it from the bark. A few orchids need loose potting; these will be discussed more fully in the plant descriptions in chapter 5. Some growers recommend soaking bark overnight, so it is easy to cut but this is not necessary.

In potting with osmunda, you follow the same procedure as for bark, except that you soak the osmunda overnight and then cut it into small chunks. Trim away any excess osmunda at the surface of the pot.

For terrestrial orchids, use an osmunda and humus mixture, and

POTTING WITH FIR BARK

Place shards in pot.

Add bark.

Tamp down bark.

Tie, stake, and label.

POTTING WITH OSMUNDA

Moisten osmunda.

Put in shards.

Add chunks of osmunda.

Tamp down.

pot the plant as you would any house plant. Label all newly potted plants with species name.

Whether you repot orchids in fir bark or osmunda, the first step is to remove the plant from its old container. Do not force or pull it out, because pressure can damage live roots. Instead, tease the plant out of the old mixture. This takes repeated gentle tugging, holding the plant in one hand, the pot with the other hand. When the plant comes loose, carefully clean away the old compost from around the roots and cut off any shriveled and brown roots.

After you pot or repot with any mixture, place the orchid where the temperature is warm (68° to 74°F.) and where there is no direct sunlight. Do not water the plant; instead, every day spray the immediate area around the plant with a very fine mist of water. Wet the pot and the edge of the surface of the compost, but never spray water directly onto the foliage or bulbs. In seven to ten days the roots will be able to absorb moisture.

ARTIFICIAL LIGHTING

Orchids do well under lights if all other cultural conditions—proper water, temperature, humidity—are present.

The initiation of buds depends not only upon the number of hours the orchids are kept under lights; temperature is important, too. You must keep accurate records, and a great deal of time and effort are necessary. No two species react the same; each has different requirements. African violets bloom under lights regardless of the number of hours the lamps are on, but this does not hold true for orchids.

Small orchids grow well under lights. Here are an Epidendrum (left, rear) and a Bletia (right, rear). (PHOTO COURTESY GENERAL ELECTRIC)

Small orchids do well under artificial light; here they are grown on a top shelf with other flowers. (PHOTO COURTESY GENERAL ELECTRIC)

If possible, use artificial light as a supplement to natural light. Many orchids initiate buds in winter. If winter days are cloudy, transfer a few plants from the growing area to the artificial light garden. Use two 40-watt Gro-Lux lamps and two standard 40-watt cool white lamps 48 inches long in a commercial metal tray with an adjustable canopy. Add a 2-inch metal liner to the tray (not absolutely necessary) for pebbles—water evaporating on the stones provides additional humidity. Because ventilation around the bottom of the pots is necessary, place redwood slats, spaced 1 inch apart, vertically over the tray. Keep the lamps on, controlled by an automatic timer, fifteen hours a day.

KEEPING ORCHIDS HEALTHY

Fertilizing orchids is always a topic of conversation at orchid meetings—and rightly so, because individual conditions govern whether plants should be fed or allowed to grow naturally. Nitrogen, a component of all fertilizers, stimulates foliage growth but often impedes flower production. Most growers do agree that orchids should have some additional feeding, but the amount and application varies from one collector to the next. In addition, you must consider the particular orchid being grown. For example, Cymbidiums and Laelias seem to require feeding, but orchids like Pleiones, Coelogynes, and Cirrhopetalums can be killed by too much fertilization.

The growing medium and size of pot also dictate whether orchids should be fed. Osmunda contains some nutrients for plant growth, but the fir bark does not. Orchids in small pots object to overfeeding—the chemicals become locked in the medium—whereas plants in larger pots can tolerate some feeding. In all cases, if you are using a regular fertilizer program for your orchids, be sure to flood plants with water once a month to leach built-up chemicals.

VIRUS

Orchids are fumigated at ports of entry, and modern insecticides have eliminated most insects. Keeping the growing area clean and inspecting new plants helps a great deal in keeping orchids healthy.

The study of virus disease in orchids goes on daily; virus disease is a vexing problem, and many of its causes and cures are still to be learned. The research is complicated by the fact that a virus can infect many different kinds of orchids and produce different symptoms in each plant. On the other hand, different viruses can produce the same symptoms in a single plant. Virus can be spread from plant to plant by infected cutting tools and insects. Infected plants, when divided and replanted, may appear perfectly healthy, but can carry a virus with them.

Virus appears on orchid plants in many different guises. Depending on the species, symptoms can be semitransparent spots or concentric rings, stippled streaks, or mottled leaves. Virus can also appear as mosaic patterns of light and dark green tissue with some black areas. Once started, the disease spreads rapidly through the plant. If you suspect that an orchid has a virus disease, discard it immediately rather than risk having the disease spread to other orchids. Fortunately, virus in orchids is only occasionally encountered in hobbyist collections.

PESTS AND DISEASE

Of the plant pests that attack plants, spider mites (red spider) are the most troublesome. They are difficult to see, and they attack the foliage and suck the plant juices, causing the leaves to become silvery. Red spiders thrive under warm, very dry conditions. Dimite, a commercial miticide, applied at weekly intervals helps to eliminate the pests.

Thrips are small chewing insects that scurry about the plant when disturbed. Some of them feed on the leaves, and others attack the flowers. Malathion is effective against them. Use according to the directions on the package.

Scale insects are particularly bothersome to orchids. There are two types of scale: soft and armored. Beetlelike, these small insects, when mature, attach themselves to orchid leaves and stems by their proboscis appendage and suck the plant juices. If not controlled, colonies develop rapidly and the plant, overwhelmed, dies. If the infestation is mild, scrub the leaves and stems with a toothbrush soaked in nicotine sulfate solution to get rid of them. If the scale has a good foothold on the plant, use Malathion to kill the adults and control hatching of the young.

Aphids are green or black small-bodied sucking insects, some with wings, others without. They can be seen moving about the plant, and they attack new growth and disfigure the foliage. Malathion controls them.

Mealybugs are cottony white sucking insects that cluster in leaf axils. You can eliminate first offenders with cotton swabs dipped in nicotine sulfate solution. Malathion is necessary to end a heavy infestation.

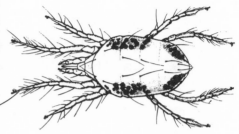

Mealybugs can sometimes be a threat to orchids but can be eliminated if caught early. (PHOTO COURTESY UNITED STATES DEPARTMENT OF AGRICULTURE [USDA])

Red spider mite occasionally is found on orchids; a miticide is usually administered to kill them. (PHOTO COURTESY USDA)

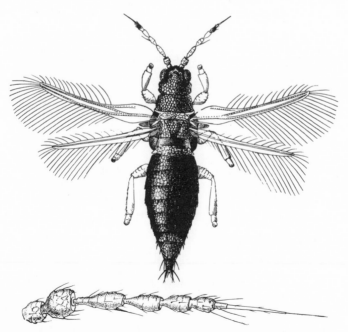

Thrips can do damage to plants and must be eliminated quickly. (PHOTO COURTESY USDA)

Slugs and snails usually do not bother orchids, because the foliage is too tough for their liking. But if they do attack, there are two excellent commercially available remedies—Slug-It and Buggetta.

Ants, although they do not damage orchids, are a nuisance. They can be controlled by sprinkling suitable ant poisons in the pots.

Springtails are tiny jumping insects that are rarely injurious to orchids, but it is best to get rid of them. Malathion is an effective control.

Fungus disease most often appears on new growth and spreads rapidly. The plant tissue turns soft, then black. Cut off all infected parts, and treat the plant with a fungicide as directed on the package.

It should be noted that Malathion is a poisonous compound; if used at all on your plants, it must be handled with great care. Keep all chemicals on high shelves, away from pets and children. And before you try the man-made chemicals consider some of the following natural means to eliminate pests on plants.

NATURAL PREVENTATIVES

There are old-fashioned ways to keep your plants free of insects, one of the best all-around insect deterrents being rubbing alcohol. Put alcohol on cotton swabs and dab the insects; mealybugs and aphids will be killed on contact.

A solution of cigarette tobacco and water (two teaspoons tobacco to one pint of water) steeped a few days can also result in success. Simply dab the solution on insects; again use a cotton swab.

Finally, a strong hosing of water directed at the insects will dis-

DIVISION

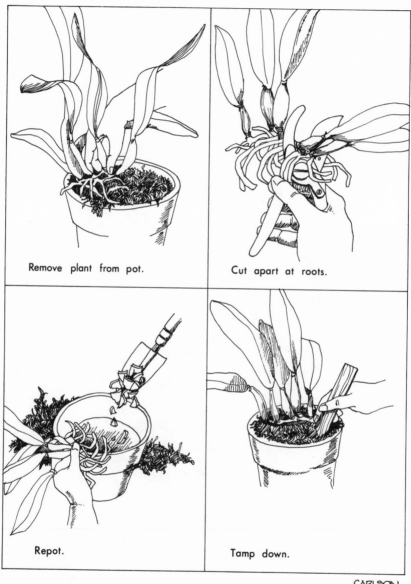

Remove plant from pot.

Cut apart at roots.

Repot.

Tamp down.

CARLSON

OFFSET DIVISION

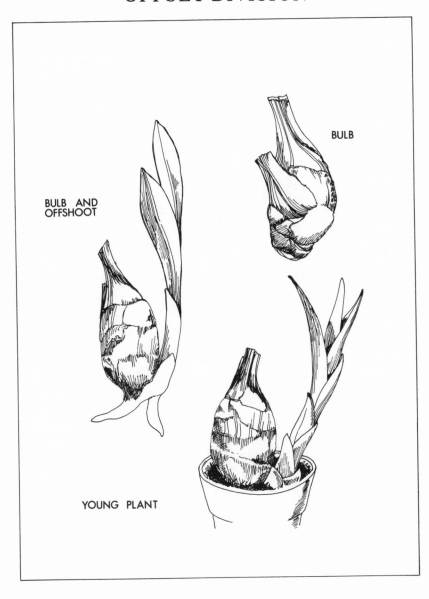

BULB

BULB AND
OFFSHOOT

YOUNG PLANT

lodge them; repeat this water treatment every day until pests disappear.

Growing Your Own Miniatures

It is possible to grow miniatures from seed, but the process is complicated and takes several years—it also takes a great deal of know-how and patience. So instead of doing it the hard way, use division to increase your number of plants. Most orchids with sympodial habits (and there are many) can be divided simply by cutting off part of the plant and potting it in a small container of fir bark.

Other orchids that do not grow in the creeping manner but have clump growth can be divided by cutting off one or two of the pseudobulbs. However, only do this with plants that have at least four or five mature bulbs. Remove one bulb that has new growth, and pot individually.

FIVE

100 Miniature Orchids to Grow

The general culture of miniature orchids and basic information concerning the plants have been outlined. Now here are over 125 miniatures, with directions for simulating specific cultural conditions. The plants were grown, with this book in mind, over a period of three years. Some were in a plant room; most were grown in a city apartment.

Each orchid is presented with specifications for light, humidity, temperature, and bloom time. There are no specific directions for feeding orchids—some mild fertilizing can certainly be undertaken during the growing seasons (in warm weather), but an excessive amount of plant food will harm most orchids. So use discretion if you decide to feed your plants. As mentioned, we have found that a mild fertilizer of 10-10-5 plant food was the best to use.

A note about plant descriptions: light requirements have been designated as Sun, Bright Light, and Shade. These conditions are equivalent to

Sun: two to three hours daily
Bright Light: not necessarily sun but direct bright light
Shade: no sun, diffused or north light.

The following orchids are only a sampling of the many miniatures you can grow.

AERANGIS

With seventy species, Aerangis is a genus of epiphytes from the Malagasy Republic and tropical Africa. Generally, the cultivated species are small orchids with long pendant spikes of white flowers. Related to Angraecums, these orchids have tough leathery foliage and do not need much attention to produce their blooms. Because most Aerangis plants bear fall or winter flowers, they surely deserve a place at the window.

The natural habitat of these orchids demands that they be grown warm and wet. Although most growers recommend warmth for Aerangis, the plants can, for a few nights, adjust to cool conditions. Grow the plants in pots of fir bark or osmunda, and keep them watered all year. Aerangis are generally available but somewhat expensive.

AERANGIS BILOBA

AERANGIS BILOBA

LIGHT: Shade
HUMIDITY: 40 percent
TEMPERATURE: 60–80°F.
FLOWERING: Fall

Pairs of broad leaves grow to about 14 inches; the plant bears an arching flower stem with about a dozen pure white glistening flowers approximately 2 inch long. The plant likes a somewhat shady place—no sun. Grow in a pot with fir bark kept quite moist but never soggy. Flowers are long-lasting and usually fragrant.

NOTE: Grow plants in fairly warm temperature; keep evenly moist.

AERANGIS FLABELLIFOLIA

LIGHT: Shade
HUMIDITY: 40 percent
TEMPERATURE: 60–80°F.
FLOWERING: Fall

The paddle-shaped leathery green leaves grow to about 14 inches; beautiful waxy white flowers are about ½ inch long. Very pretty. Grow in a pot of fir bark; keep evenly moist. Provide bright light but keep plant out of sun.

NOTE: Plant likes warmth.

AERANGIS KIRKII

LIGHT: Shade
HUMIDITY: 40 percent
TEMPERATURE: 60–80°F.
FLOWERING: Fall

This plant has fans of green paddle-shaped leaves; Flowers usually grow on drooping stems, are white and about ½ inch long. The flowers resemble birds in flight. Grow in an airy, shady place in a pot with fir bark. Mist frequently. Don't allow water to stand in crowns of leaves.

NOTE: Plant needs a shady but moist place.

AERANGIS RHODOSTICTA

LIGHT: Bright
HUMIDITY: 60 percent
TEMPERATURE: 60–75°F.
FLOWERING: Winter

This plant has 3-inch long dark green leaves, and 5-inch flower spikes are borne at the base of the plant. Flowers are creamy-white and star-shaped with an orange-red column. Grow this plant in a

(Continued)

pot with fir bark. Do not overwater; the plant does well in terrariums.

NOTE: After flowers fade, let the plant rest somewhat dry for a few weeks. Then in spring, when new growth starts, resume routine watering.

Aerangis rhodosticta
(PHOTO BY ROY CRAFTON)

AERANTHES

Aeranthes is a small genus of orchids of the Malagasy Republic. With straplike leaves, they produce remarkable chartreuse flowers, more curious than beautiful. The flowers, on long wiry scapes (Stems), are borne from the base of the plant; they are triangular with a blunt spur. Old flower stalks will bloom again, so do not cut them. Pot this orchid in fir bark; water heavily all year. Bloom can appear in any season. Only one species is generally available, better suited perhaps for the greenhouse than the windowsill because it needs high humidity.

AERANTHES ARACHNITES

LIGHT: Bright
HUMIDITY: 50 percent
TEMPERATURE: 65–80°F.
FLOWERING: Fall

This plant has light green, linear, 8- to 10-inch-long leaves. Emerald green cup-shaped flowers appear on 12-inch-long, thin, wiry scapes that are borne from the base of the plant. The flowers are most peculiar: they are cup-shaped but resemble a small insect. The flowers hold a small amount of liquid in their throats for several weeks. Grow the plant in a pot with fir bark; keep moist.

NOTE: Overexposure to sun will burn the leaves and turn them yellow.

AERIDES

This is a genus of sixty species of epiphytic orchids native to tropical Asia. The plants have diversified growth patterns, and within the group are some fine miniatures for the home.

The small members of this family require a bright, airy location, and although classified as warm plants, they do grow and bloom in coolness, too—55°F. at night. Water these orchids heavily while they grow, but let them dry out somewhat for about a month after they flower, keeping them barely moist. Grow Aerides in a sunny place; pot in fir bark or osmunda. The plants are widely available.

AERIDES CRASSIFOLIUM

LIGHT: Sun

HUMIDITY: 40 percent

TEMPERATURE: 60–75°F.

FLOWERING: Spring/summer

The leaves of this plant are 6 to 9 inches long; it has pendant spikes, sometimes 10 inches long, crowded with many fragrant purple flowers about 1 inch in diameter. This is a beautiful and dependable orchid that is in color in June. Grow in fir bark in clay pots. Do not overwater.

NOTE: Grows well in a sunny place and needs plenty of water in early spring. Mist with tepid water to maintain good humidity.

AERIDES
(SEDIREA) JAPONICUM

LIGHT: Sun

HUMIDITY: 40 percent

TEMPERATURE: 60–75°F.

FLOWERING: Fall

This is perhaps the smallest species in the genus Aerides. It has leaves only 3 to 4 inches long, with an attractively branched flower spike. The fragrant blooms are white and marked with red. The plant can be grown on cork bark or in a small pot with fir bark; do not overwater.

NOTE: Keep evenly moist all year—give bright light or sun.

AERIDES MACULOSUM

LIGHT: Bright
HUMIDITY: 30 percent
TEMPERATURE: 55–65°F.
FLOWERING: Summer

This plant seldom grows taller than 9 inches. The pleasantly scented light rose flowers have purple spots and are carried on a drooping stem. A lovely summer-flowering orchid. Grow in a pot with fir bark.

NOTE: Place in bright light—sun is not necessary. Keep growing medium quite moist all year; maintain good air circulation.

ANOECTOCHILUS

A genus of terrestrial orchids, Anoectochilus are plants grown for their exquisite foliage rather than flowers. They are called Jewel orchids, and there are about twenty species native to India. The plants are difficult to cultivate because they require high humidity and careful watering—too much water causes rot. Most of the Jewel orchids are small—to about 14 inches—and, if you have time for them, make handsome additions to the collection. It would be hard to find more brilliantly colored foliage.

ANOECTOCHILUS ROXBURGHII

LIGHT: Bright
HUMIDITY: 70 percent
TEMPERATURE: 70–85°F.
FLOWERING: Summer

This plant has rich dark green leaves veined with gold; the small flowers are tawny red. Grow in pots; use equal parts of soil and fir bark; plant requires high humidity and careful watering. Too much moisture can cause rot. The stems are brittle, so be careful when handling the plant.

NOTE: Plant needs heat and humidity to thrive.

ANGRAECUM

Angraecums, mostly native to South Africa and Malagasy, are generally large plants; however, the genus also includes some splendid miniatures—perhaps the best small orchids known. The plants are ideal for the home or greenhouse. They have fan-shaped growth with leathery dark green leaves and larger white flowers.

These diminutive orchids need warmth—60°F at night—and a moist atmosphere when growing. Place them where there is some sunlight, and, most important, be sure there is good air circulation in the growing area. Grow Angraecums in osmunda or fir bark.

ANGRAECUM COMPACTUM

ANGRAECUM COMPACTUM

LIGHT: Bright
HUMIDITY: 20 percent
TEMPERATURE: 55–80°F.
FLOWERING: Fall

Only 5 inches high, this plant has 2-inch fragrant white flowers. Grow the plant in fir bark or on fern slabs; keep quite moist.

NOTE: Handsome orchid that can tolerate some coolness if necessary.

ANGRAECUM FALCATUM

LIGHT: Bright
HUMIDITY: 40 percent
TEMPERATURE: 58–80°F.
FLOWERING Summer

This plant has 2- to 4-inch long glossy, deep green, linear leaves. The fragrant, pure, white, waxy flowers with thin 2-inch long spurs appear in clusters. Grow the plant in a pot with fir bark, keep moist.

NOTE: Always provide good air circulation.

ASCOCENTRUM

Sometimes called Saccolabium, the genus Ascocentrum has nine epiphytic species from India, Burma, and Malaysia. With leathery leaves, they are not much to look at until they bloom, but then they are spectacular. The flower colors are vibrant—orange, red, or rose-purple—with as many as thirty blooms to a spike, and the blooms last for several weeks. Keep plants quite moist but never allow fir bark to become soggy.

ASCOCENTRUM AMPULLACEUM

LIGHT: Bright
HUMIDITY: 50 percent
TEMPERATURE: 55–75°F.
FLOWERING: Fall

This plant has 3½-inch-long dark green leaves and clusters of bright rose-carmine flowers with a spurred yellow lip. Grow it in a small pot with fir bark.

NOTE: A most enjoyable and very good house plant. Water two to three times a week on sunny days, less on cloudy days.

ASOCENTRUM CURVIFOLIUM

LIGHT: Bright
HUMIDITY: 40 percent
TEMPERATURE: 55–65°F.
FLOWERING: Fall

The green leathery leaves are 8 to 10 inches long, and the plant has cinnabar red 1-inch flowers. Grow in a pot with fir bark; keep evenly moist.

NOTE: Avoid temperature fluctuation. Best to keep in one location.

ASCOCENTRUM MICRANTHUM

LIGHT: Sun
HUMIDITY: 40 percent
TEMPERATURE: 55–75°F.
FLOWERING: Summer

The 2-inch, light green, leathery leaves have notched ends. Flowers appear between the leaf axils on 3-inch-long spikes, branching into many spikes bearing clusters of ¼-inch white flowers with lavender markings. The flower looks like a small winged insect. Grow in a pot with fir bark, keep evenly moist.

NOTE: Plant can tolerate some coolness; needs good humidity.

ASCOCENTRUM MINIATUM

LIGHT: Sun
HUMIDITY: 30 percent
TEMPERATURE: 55–75°F.
FLOWERING: Fall

This small epiphyte has a short erect stem clothed with ranks of 2- to 4-inch-long linear leaves, and there are short clusters of small but bright red-orange flowers. Grow in pots with fir bark; keep evenly moist.

NOTE: No special requirements.

ASCOCENTRUM PUMILUM

LIGHT: Bright
HUMIDITY: 45 percent
TEMPERATURE: 55–75°F.
FLOWERING: Winter

This plant has ½-inch-long needlelike green leaves and ½-inch flowers. The sepals and petals are lavender to pink, with a straight ⅛-inch spur, a green inner throat, and a deep lavender dot above the throat. Grow on moist cork bark.

NOTE: Spray plant every few days to encourage good humidity. Give good air circulation.

BRASSAVOLA

Brassavola is a genus of a few epiphytic orchids distributed mainly through Central America. The plants have leaves that are terete (pencil-like) and hardly look like orchids. Flowers are white and heavily scented. There are only two species in this group suitable for windowsill growing and generally easy to bring to bloom. *Brassavola nodosa,* in particular, is well worth its space at the window.

BRASSAVOLA GLAUCA

LIGHT: Bright
HUMIDITY: 30 percent
TEMPERATURE: 55–75°F.
FLOWERING: Summer

A plant with 5-inch dark green leathery leaves, *B. glauca* has handsome, fragrant, white flowers; the texture is almost crystalline. The plant needs plenty of moisture in warm weather—at other times, it can be grown somewhat dry. It is best cultivated on slabs or small branches.

NOTE: Do not overwater in cold weather.

BRASSAVOLA NODOSA

LIGHT: Sun

HUMIDITY: 40 percent

TEMPERATURE: 60–75°F.

FLOWERING: Variable

This plant has terete, almost succulent-type leaves; flowers are to 2 inches, white and fragrant. Grow the plant in clay pots with fir bark; keep quite moist.

NOTE: Repot only every third year; plant resents root disturbance.

Brassavola nodosa (PHOTO BY J. KRAMER)

BROUGHTONIA

Broughtonia, a genus with only one species, is closely allied to Epidendrum. This epiphyte from Jamaica should certainly be more popular, because it bears vivid red flowers and needs little care. Even a small plant has four or five bloom spikes, each with several flowers.

Although growers recommend heat and high humidity for Broughtonias, my plant was in full color outdoors from April until late June. Night temperature of 58°F. helped rather than hinderd its bloom. It was in direct sunlight most of the day, and coast breezes kept it almost always dry.

BROUGHTONIA SANGUINEA

LIGHT: Bright/ Sun
HUMIDITY: 45 percent
TEMPERATURE: 55–80°F.
FLOWERING: Spring

This plant produces a large and irregular pseudobulb that has one or two 4- to 6-inch-long green leaves. The flowers are roundish and flattened and overall crimson. Grow the plant on bark or in small pots with fir bark.

NOTE: Keep the temperature above 55°F., or you may lose leaves and flower buds may drop.

BULBOPHYLLUM

This is a large genus of 2,000 species distributed through the tropical and subtropical parts of the world. Eiphytic plants, Bulbophyllums are characterized by small, intricate flowers that are handsome or curious. Most of the plants have pseudobulbs on a creeping rhizome with a solitary leaf, and a great many are small plants, to about 6 inches high. The flowers come in every imaginable color except blue and black; greenish -brown is the color seen most frequently.

Because there are so many species in the genus, it is difficult to give concrete cultural guidelines. Generally, grow Bulbophyllums warm (65°F. at night), and keep them moist all year. Pot in osmunda or mount of fir bark slabs in the sun.

BULBOPHYLLUM BARBIGERUM

LIGHT: Sun
HUMIDITY: 40 percent
TEMPERATURE: 65–75°F.
FLOWERING: Summer

This plant has 2- to 3-inch green leathery leaves and produces an intricate flower, with tufts of purple-brown hairs. There are several blooms to a scape. The plant is best grown on moist slabs.

NOTE: Generally easy to grow indoors. Keep somewhat dry. Needs good air circulation.

BULBOPHYLLUM LEMNISCATOIDES

LIGHT: Sun
HUMIDITY: 40 percent
TEMPERATURE: 65–75°F.
FLOWERING: Fall/Winter

This orchid has 2-inch-long dark green leathery leaves and small, dark purplish flowers. The sepals have white hairs and a trailing ribbon appendage that is white and spotted red. The plant is best grown on moist slabs or a branch.

NOTE: Keep plant evenly moist—likes humidity—otherwise easy to grow. The trailing ribbons make it a true oddity of nature.

BULBOPHYLLUM LOBBII

LIGHT: Bright/Shade
HUMIDITY: 30 percent
TEMPERATURE: 55–75°F.
FLOWERING: Variable

This plant—somewhat large to be considered dwarf, but so very pretty—grows to about 14 inches. It has dark green leaves and solitary copper colored hooded flowers, usualy scented. Keep evenly moist all year; pot with fir bark. The plant is rare, and difficult to find, but worth the search.

NOTE: Direct sunlight will harm plant.

BULBOPHYLLUM LOBBII

BULBOPHYLLUM MEDUSAE
(Cirrhopetalum medusae)

LIGHT: Bright

HUMIDITY: 40 percent

TEMPERATURE: 60–80°F.

FLOWERING: Summer

The plant has 5-inch-long leathery leaves; the flowers are dense heads of straw-colored blooms. Now available for the first time at a modest price, this orchid is another beauty. Grow in fir bark in pots, keep quite dry.

NOTE: Do not grow too wet—prefers a dry medium. Keep warm and mist frequently.

BULBOPHYLLUM MORPHOLOGORUM

LIGHT: Shade

HUMIDITY: 20 percent

TEMPERATURE: 55–75°F.

FLOWERING: Usually fall

The thrusting head of this plant produces several hundred small blooms that are yellowish-brown with brown spots. The flower cluster is sometimes 6 inches long. This is a most unusual orchid— only occasionally offered, but worth searching for. Grow in fir bark in a pot; keep somewhat dry.

NOTE: *B. morphologorum* prefers a shady, moist place. Do not disturb once the plant is growing well.

BULBOPHYLLUM MEDUSAE

BULBOPHYLLUM ODORATISSIMUM

LIGHT: Bright
HUMIDITY: 60 percent
TEMPERATURE: 60–75°F.
FLOWERING: Fall

This epiphyte has small ovoid pseudobulbs. Each pseudobulb produces one 2- to 6-inch-long, medium green, leathery leaf. The yellowish or pale purplish-brown flowers are 3 to 4 inches long and striped and netted with dark purple; the lip is crimson-purple. This orchid can be grown in a pot with a mixture of fir bark and osmunda.

NOTE: Keep growing medium quite moist. The plant needs good humidity—spray with water frequently.

BULBOPHYLLUM SAUNDERSONII

LIGHT: Bright
HUMIDITY: 60 percent
TEMPERATURE: 60–75°F.
FLOWERING: Summer

This plant bears swollen pseudobulbs, each having 2- to 4-inch light green leaves with white specks. Twenty or more flowers appear on a 4- to 5-inch spike; the petals are burgundy and the sepals are light green with tiny burgundy specks. The yellow to light brown lip moves with the wind. Grow *B. saundersonii* on a moist slab; keep the plant moderately moist.

NOTE: Mist plant often.

BULBOPHYLLUM TRANSARISANENSE

LIGHT: Bright
HUMIDITY: 60 percent
TEMPERATURE: 55–75°F
FLOWERING: Summer

This orchid's fibrous roots produce pseudobulbs, each with one 5-inch-long green leaf. The flower stems appear from the base of the bulbs. The flowers begin to open in May; the sepals and petals are light green, and a large spotted lip protrudes from the center of the flower. Grow the plant on moist cork bark. Submerge the cork bark in water several times a week, and mist a lot (do *not* wet the flowers).

NOTE: No special requirements.

Bulbophyllum transarisanense

CALANTHE

Calanthe is a large genus of mostly terrestrial orchids widely distributed through Asia and China with some from the West Indies and Central America. The plants are somewhat unusual in the orchid family because they grow from a tuberlike rhizome and can be treated in the same manner as Gloxinias or other tuberous plants—grown for a season (three months or so) and then rested in a brown paper bag in cool temperatures until ready to plant again. Calanthes are very desirable because the flowers are extremely handsome and bloom in the winter.

Calanthe vestita (PHOTO BY J. KRAMER)

CALANTHE VESTITA

LIGHT: Bright
HUMIDITY: 30 percent
TEMPERATURE: 55–75°F.
FLOWERING: Winter

This plant generally has deciduous papery green leaves; the flowers are large for the size of the plant—several to a long scape—and are usually pink or white. Grow in a pot with equal parts of soil and fir bark; after flowering allow the plant to rest in a cool (50°F.), dry place for about three to four months—then repot and start again.

NOTE: Must have definite rest period.

CAPANEMIA

Capanemia is a small genus of about fifteen species from Brazil. The plants are about 4 inches tall and produce small but lovely flowers, delightfully scented. Plants grow well in average home temperatures and with ample sunshine and plenty of water all year. Pot in fir bark. These plants will reward you with an abundance of flowers for little cost.

CAPANEMIA AUSTRALIS

LIGHT: Bright
HUMIDITY: 30 percent
TEMPERATURE: 55–75°F.
FLOWERING: Summer

With needlelike leaves and minute white flowers, these are charming plants that bloom on and off through spring and summer. From Brazil, the plants like a somewhat warm place and are best grown in fir bark in pots; keep evenly moist.

NOTE: No special requirements.

CAPANEMIA MICROMEIRA

LIGHT: Bright
HUMIDITY: 40 percent
TEMPERATURE: 55–75°F.
FLOWERING: Winter

Leaves are ½- to 1-inch-long, needlelike and green. The flowers are borne alongside the pseudobulbs on a ¼-inch-long spike; flowers have a yellow inset lip. Grow the plant on cork bark or in a pot with a mixture of fir bark and osmunda; keep moist.

NOTE: This plant needs attention just to keep from being overlooked because it is so small. Does not like overly moist conditions. Spray with tepid water frequently.

CATTLEYA

Cattleya is the most popular genus in the Orchidaceae; from it we get the handsome corsage flowers. But also included in the group, mostly from South America, are some—not too many—small gems. The leaves are straplike and leathery green and even the miniature flowers resemble their larger cousins. Generally, these miniatures bloom in spring or in fall. Use fir bark as a growing medium and small clay pots, and keep medium quite moist all year. Cattleyas require good sunlight to bloom; without it flowers are sparse. Keep humidity at about 40 percent. Repot only when absolutely necessary.

CATTLEYA CITRINA

LIGHT: Sun
HUMIDITY: 40 percent
TEMPERATURE: 65–80°F.
FLOWERING: Variable

This plant has small pseudobulbs and light green leaves about 5 inches long. The orchid grows in a pendant fashion and does best on a moist slab of wood or a branch. Flowers are brilliant yellow— a dazzling sight—but only very mature plants bloom. It was four years before the plant in our collection yielded its harvest of beauty.

NOTE: *Cattleya citrina* requires excellent sun—grow the plant somewhat dry all year. Not easy, but certainly worth the effort.

CATTLEYA WALKERIANA

LIGHT: Bright/Sun

HUMIDITY: 40 percent

TEMPERATURE: 55–75°F.

FLOWERING: Winter

With solitary green leathery leaves to 5 inches, this orchid does not bloom from the leaf area but, rather, from the side of the bulb. The exquisite magenta flowers are large for the plant—about 2 inches across—and slightly fragrant. Grow the plant in pots with fir bark. This is one of the best miniatures available.

NOTE: Plant likes conditions that are somewhat cool and moist, but needs sunlight to bloom.

CIRRHOPETALUM

Closely allied to Bulbophyllums, and often confused with them, Cirrhopetalum is a large genus of orchids from diversified parts of the globe. Perhaps the greatest number are from Borneo and New Guinea. Many species have brightly colored flowers; while they are small and usually of singular growth, the flowers are set close together in clusters to form patterns such as an ellipse or a circle. They are stylish and decorative.

CIRRHOPETALUM CORNUTUM

LIGHT: Bright
HUMIDITY: 40 percent
TEMPERATURE: 62–75°F.
FLOWERING: Summer

This plant produces 5-inch-long green leaves. Flowers are ¾-inch long; the sepals are yellowish-green, and the petals are covered with tiny burgundy specks. The small inset lip has purple specks on top and white on its underside, with large deep purple spots. The flower is shaped something like a small moth or butterfly. Grow the plant in a pot with fir bark. Water it two or three times a week.

NOTE: Flowers are pot huggers and last for weeks. Easy to grow and a good house plant.

CIRRHOPETALUM CUMINGII

LIGHT: Bright
HUMIDITY: 40 percent
TEMPERATURE: 55–75°F.
FLOWERING: Winter

This plant has 1- to 2-inch green leathery leaves; the brilliant red and pink flowers are in the shape of a half circle. Grow the plant mounted on cork bark or tree fern slabs. Keep evenly moist all year.

NOTE: Easy indoor plant that grows well with little attention.

CIRRHOPETALUM CUMINGII

CIRRHOPETALUM GRACILLIMUM

LIGHT: Bright
HUMIDITY: 30 percent
TEMPERATURE: 60–80°F.
FLOWERING: Summer

This orchid typically has 1- to 2-inch leathery leaves; the slender scapes rise above the foliage and carry very pretty crimson-red flowers. Grow the plant in small pots with fir bark; keep evenly moist all year.

NOTE: Does well at east or west windows.

CIRRHOPETALUM GUTTALATUM

LIGHT: Bright
HUMIDITY: 55 percent
TEMPERATURE: 62–75°F.
FLOWERING: Fall/Winter

This plant bears 1½-inch pseudobulbs with 2- to 3-inch-long glossy dark green leaves. Flowers appear in a cluster on a wire-like stem; they are cream with tiny red dots. Grow the plant in a pot with fir bark. Keep bark quite moist.

NOTE: Needs heat to prosper—sun not necessary; a lovely plant.

CIRRHOPETALUM LISHANENSIS

LIGHT: Bright
HUMIDITY: 40 percent
TEMPERATURE: 62–75°F.
FLOWERING: Fall

This plant bears pseudobulbs, each with one light green, 1½-inch-long leaf. There are ten flowers per cluster; the sepals and petals are light green, with veinlike markings on their outer sides and an extended white hairy edge. A 1- to 3-inch-long light green needle-like spur and red-orange lip make this a most interesting flower. Grow the plant on moist cork bark.

NOTE: An easy-to-care for plant; dependable.

CIRRHOPETALUM LONGISSIMUM

LIGHT: Bright
HUMIDITY: 30 percent
TEMPERATURE: 60–80°F.
FLOWERING: Summer

This miniature has small 2-inch-long leathery leaves; the plant produces an ice-cream pink inflorescence with elongated petals and lip. Grow in a pot with fir bark. Keep evenly moist. A remarkable species.

NOTE: Grow in same way as *C. gracillimum*.

Cirrhopetalum maculosum

CIRRHOPETALUM MACULOSUM

LIGHT: Bright

HUMIDITY: 45 percent

TEMPERATURE: 62–75°F.

FLOWERING: Fall

With swollen pseudobulbs, this plant produces one 2½-inch-long semiglossy green leaf and small greenish-brown hood-shaped flowers. Grow the plant on a cork or wood slab or in a pot with chopped osmunda. Grow evenly moist all year.

NOTE: This orchid is easy to grow.

CIRRHOPETALUM MASTERSIANUM

LIGHT: Bright

HUMIDITY: 30 percent

TEMPERATURE: 55–75°F.

FLOWERING: Winter

With solitary leaves and beautiful flowers, *C. mastersianum* bears small brownish-orange flowers in a most unusual semi-arc arrangement. Plants do best on slabs but may also be grown in fir bark in pots. Keep evenly moist all year. This orchid bears flowers on and off through the winter.

NOTE: No special requirements.

Cirrhopetalum mastersianum (PHOTO BY JOYCE WILSON)

CIRRHOPETALUM ORNATISSIMUM

LIGHT: Bright
HUMIDITY: 40 percent
TEMPERATURE: 62–75°F.
FLOWERING: Fall

This rhizome produces pseudobulbs, each with one light green, leathery, 1- to 3-inch-long leaf; the flowers are pink striped with purple. Grow the plant on cork bark. Submerge the plant into a sink of water several times a week if possible.

NOTE: Provide good air circulation and mist often.

CIRRHOPETALUM ROXBURGHII

LIGHT: Bright
HUMIDITY: 40 percent
TEMPERATURE: 55–75°F.
FLOWERING: Summer/Fall

With small typical single green leaves and an umbrella of pink flowers, C. *roxburghii* is most dainty. Grow it on cork bark or tree fern fiber and keep evenly moist all year.

NOTE: A very pretty plant; needs somewhat cooler conditions than most Cirrhopetalums.

CIRRHOPETALUM WATSONIANUM

LIGHT: Bright
HUMIDITY: 50 percent
TEMPERATURE: 62–75°F.
FLOWERING: Variable

The plant has 1-inch-long pseudobulbs, each having one 1-inch-long, glossy, deep green leaf. The flowers are a delicate pink. Grow the plant in a pot with a mixture of finely ground osmunda and fir bark. Submerge into a sink of water every two days.

NOTE: This plant needs humidity; it also grows well on osmunda; spray it often.

COMPARETTIA

Comparettias are native to Cuba, Mexico, and the South American Andes. Only recently available, these dwarf epiphytes have fleshy leaves and dramatic sprays of scarlet or orange flowers that are quite large for the size of the plant.

Keep these orchids somewhat dry in a bright location, and provide good humidity. Most grow well on small blocks of wood; however, they also can be grown in 3-inch pots. Plants can tolerate coolness and do best in a night temperature of about 55°F.

COMPARETTIA FALCATA

COMPARETTIA FALCATA

LIGHT: Shade/Bright
HUMIDITY: 30 percent
TEMPERATURE: 55–75°F.
FLOWERING: Fall/Winter

This is one of the prettiest orchids available, with 4-inch leaves and an arching stalk of vivid rose-magenta flowers. Grow in clay pots with fir bark; do not overwater.

NOTE: Easily grown; needs even moisture and good humidity. Highly recommended. Flowers open gradually over a period of time.

COMPARETTIA SPECIOSA

LIGHT: Shade/Bright
HUMIDITY: 30 percent
TEMPERATURE: 55–75°F.
FLOWERING: Fall/Winter

This orchid is similar to *C. falcata* but has bright yellowish-orange flowers. Grow on cork bark or tree fern slabs.

NOTE: Grow same as *C. falcata*.

CYPRIPEDIUM

Cypripedium, also called Paphiopedilum, is a genus of fity species of Asiatic origin. Cypripedium hybrids are popular as cut flowers, since they are large, showy, and long-lasting. The blooms are weirdly fascinating and come in lurid color combinations. The waxy inflorescence often seems more artificial than real. Small species are popular with collectors; they are handsome and adapt well to windowsill culture. The plants are mainly terrestrial. The family is complex, with some species requiring warm conditions and others needing coolness.

The genus is without pseudobulbs and has dark green or mottled strap foliage in a handsome fan formation attached to a fleshy rhizome. The flower spike comes from the center of the leaves and carries one or several flowers that last five to seven weeks on the plant.

CYPRIPEDIUM ANG-THONG

LIGHT: Bright
HUMIDITY: 50 percent
TEMPERATURE: 55–80°F.
FLOWERING: Summer

The 3- to 5-inch-long, semiglossy, deep green, leathery leaves have light markings. The white flowers appear from the crown of the plant. Purple markings dot the sepals and petals, and the large cupped lip has a yellow center above it. Grow the plant in pots with fir bark; keep evenly moist all year.

NOTE: Let this orchid dry out between waterings; provide warm temperatures.

CYPRIPEDIUM SPICERIANUM

CYPRIPEDIUM EXUL

LIGHT: Bright/Shade
HUMIDITY: 40 percent
TEMPERATURE: 55–75°F.
FLOWERING: Fall

The 10-inch-long semiglossy leaves are leathery. The yellow-green flowers are spotted brown at the base, and the lip is brownish yellow. Grow the plant in a pot with a mixture of fir bark, wood chips, and some perlite.

NOTE: Unusual; a good plant for a shady place. It sometimes blooms a second time in late fall.

CYPRIPEDIUM SPICERIANUM

LIGHT: Bright
HUMIDITY: 30 percent
TEMPERATURE: 50–75°F.
FLOWERING: Summer

This orchid has green leaves and a single flower from each growth. The bloom is glistening white, green at the base with a purple stripe down the center. Petals are pale green and marked with purple. Grow the plant in fir bark in a pot; keep evenly moist all year. Flowers last for several weeks.

NOTE: Plant likes cool conditions.

Dendrobium

Dendrobium is among the largest of all orchid genera, with more than 1,500 species widely distributed throughout the world. Many are from India, Burma, and Ceylon, others from parts of China and Japan, and a great number are native to Australia and the Philippines. The species vary greatly in shape and habit; most have cane-type growth; all produce beautiful flowers.

The plants need about four hours of sun a day and abundant watering until growth is mature. Then, to encourage flower spikes, a rest period of three to four weeks without water is in order. After flowering, allow a complete rest of five to seven weeks without water. Repot only when needed, about every second year.

DENDROBIUM ARACHNITES

LIGHT: Bright/Sun
HUMIDITY: 50 percent
TEMPERATURE: 55–75°F.
FLOWERING: Fall

This is a thick-stemmed Dendrobium with alternate 2- to 4-inch-long green leaves. The bright orange flowers' sepals and petals appear in pairs on a leafless stem. Grow the plant in a pot with chopped osmunda and fir bark.

NOTE: This plant grows best in good humidity with once-a-week watering and ample air circulation.

DENDROBIUM CAPILLIPES

LIGHT: Bright
HUMIDITY: 40 percent
TEMPERATURE: 55–75°F.
FLOWERING: Fall

The 2- to 3-inch-long, semiglossy, medium green leaves are alternately ranked on a succulent stem. The round, rich yellow flowers have red stripes in their throats. Grow in small pots with fir bark.

NOTE: Grow this plant in good humidity. Water it once a week and provide good air circulation.

DENDROBIUM LODDIGESII

LIGHT: Bright
HUMIDITY: 50 percent
TEMPERATURE: 55–75°F.
FLOWERING: Fall

This plant is a trailer, growing from long rhizomes. It stems out, with alternate 1- and 2-inch-long light green leaves. The 2-inch flowers are borne on creeping stems. The pink sepals and petals have a most interesting lip covered with tiny hairs. On the edge of the lip the hairs are faded pink; inside the lip, all the way to the

(*Continued*)

center, the hairs are yellow. Grow in a pot with chopped osmunda, or fir bark.

NOTE: Keep the potting mixture barely moist. Always provide ample air circulation or flowers will mildew. The flowers last for several weeks.

Dendrobium loddigesii

DENDROBIUM MARGUERITACEUM

LIGHT: Bright
HUMIDITY: 40 percent
TEMPERATURE: 60–70°F.
FLOWERING: Summer

The succulentlike stems have alternate 1- to 2-inch-long green leaves. The flowers are white, with a large white lip that has deep orange-red markings on its throat to the center of the lip, which is tinged yellow. This Dendrobium grows best on cork bark kept barely moist.

NOTE: Grow the plant somewhat dry between waterings.

DENDROBIUM NAKAHARAI

LIGHT: Low
HUMIDITY: 50 percent
TEMPERATURE: 70–75°F.
FLOWERING: Summer

The glossy dark green leaves are 1½ inches long; the sepals are yellow, and the petals have a reddish-brown lip. Grow this plant mounted on cork bark.

NOTE: This is a pleasing and small orchid that is easy to grow. No special attention needed.

DENDROBIUM PARISHII

LIGHT: Bright/Sun
HUMIDITY: 50 percent
TEMPERATURE: 50–75°F.
FLOWERING: Fall

This plant has 5-inch-long light green leaves. The sepals and petals are lavender; the semiruffled lip has deep violet tones on either side of its throat. Grow the plant in a pot with a mixture of fir bark and wood chips; keep somewhat dry.

NOTE: New leaves begin to form in the late winter from the base of older growth. Grow the plant with good air circulation, bright light, and high humidity.

Dendrochilum

A genus of few species from the Philippines, Dendrochilum includes one the most popular small orchids cultivated: *D. filiforme*. This plant, with bright green clusters of leaves, is handsome even when not in bloom. Some plants will bloom twice a year and, in general, are very easy to grow. They need little attention.

DENDROCHILUM FILIFORME

LIGHT: Bright
HUMIDITY: 30 percent
TEMPERATURE: 55–75°F.
FLOWERING: Variable

This plant has slender pseudobulbs and long narrow leaves to 12 inches. The flowers grow in a perfect pattern on a long drooping stem—flowers are golden white. Grow in a pot with fir bark kept evenly moist all year.

NOTE: Repot only when absolutely necessary—about every third year.

DENDROCHILUM
FILIFORME

DORITAENOPSIS

This is one of the few hyrbids in this book but it deserves mention because the plants are so beautiful and offer so much color. A cross between *Phalaenopsis lindenii* and *Doritis pulcherrima,* the plants have the typical, somewhat leathery, leaf and bear wands of open-faced, usually pink or lavender flowers in summer or fall. These Phalaenopsis hybrids require even moisture all year and somewhat warm conditions.

Doritaenopsis 'Asahi'

DORITAENOPSIS 'ASAHI'

LIGHT: Bright
HUMIDITY: 30 percent
TEMPERATURE: 60–80°F.
FLOWERING: Summer

The leaves of this plant grow to 4 inches and are somewhat leathery in texture; the flower spike is about 6 inches long, with handsome lavender flowers ½ inch across. The plant is very pretty. Grow in fir bark in small pots; keep evenly moist.

NOTE: This hybrid is available from Oak Hill Gardens (see list of suppliers at end of book).

EPIDENDRUM

Epidendrum is one of the larger orchid genera, with about 1,000 species distributed mainly through Central America, Mexico, Brazil, and tropical America. These plants may be terrestrial or epiphytic and are variable in form. Some have globose or hard egg-shaped pseudobulbs, some have stemlike pseudobulbs, and others are without pseudobulbs and have flexible or reedlike stems. Flowers come in every color imaginable and many species bloom throughout the year.

Epidendrums require direct sunlight and tight, hard potting in osmunda or fir bark. Plenty of water is necessary while plants are in active growth and until flowering. Then a pronounced rest of three to five weeks is needed with very little water. In dull months, waterings also can be decreased somewhat.

Epidendrum polybulbon
(PHOTO BY JOYCE WILSON)

EPIDENDRUM MICROBULBON

LIGHT: Bright
HUMIDITY: 50 percent
TEMPERATURE: 62–75°F.
FLOWERING: Winter

This plant has two 3-inch-long, glossy dark green, linear leaves. The flowers are small, and generally white, but may be suffused with pink. Grow the plant in a pot with fir bark.

NOTE: Provide ample humidity; keep moist all year.

EPIDENDRUM POLYBULBON
(Dinema polybulbon)

LIGHT: Bright
HUMIDITY: 50 percent
TEMPERATURE: 62–75°F.
FLOWERING: Winter

Tiny pseudobulbs, each with two leaves rarely exceeding 2¾ inches
in length, characterize this plant. The ¾-inch solitary flowers are
brownish with yellow margins and have a pure white lip. Grow in
a pot with fir bark.

NOTE: This plant grows well if given sufficient humidity. Do not
overwater.

Epidendrum porpax

EPIDENDRUM PORPAX

LIGHT: Bright
HUMIDITY: 30 percent
TEMPERATURE: 60–80°F.
FLOWERING: Summer/Fall

This orchid has shiny green 2-inch leaves and single greenish flowers with a red-brown lip—many flowers to a plant. Grow in a pot with fir bark kept evenly moist. The plant is a very famous and popular orchid.

NOTE: Also known as *Neolehmannia porpax*.

GASTROCHILUS

Gastrochilus, a genus of about fifteen species of epiphytic orchids, is native to Japan and the areas from the Himalayas to Indonesia. With leathery leaves and fleshy roots, the plants produce stunning flowers in clusters. The clusters are generally borne at the base of the plant and make a pretty bouquet.

Warmth and sunshine bring Gastrochilus to bloom. Pot them in osmunda or fir bark, and keep them moist all year except immediately after they flower, at which time a short rest of about three weeks is desirable. These are easy plants to grow at windowsills or in the greenhouse. Recent introductions, these plants no doubt will be seen more often in the near future.

Gastrochilus bellinus

GASTROCHILUS BELLINUS

LIGHT: Bright/Sun
HUMIDITY: 45 percent
TEMPERATURE: 50–75°F.
FLOWERING: Summer

This plant has 5- to 7-inch-long leathery green leaves. The flowers are mustard yellow, and the petals have brownish-red markings. The ruffled white lip is cup-shaped with purple specks and splotches. Grow the plant in a pot with fir bark.

NOTE: Keep evenly moist; the orchid produces long-lasting flowers.

GASTROCHILUS CALCEOLARIS

LIGHT: BRIGHT/SUN
HUMIDITY: 40 percent
TEMPERATURE: 60–75°F.
FLOWERING: Winter

This orchid has 8-inch-long green leaves. The flower spikes are produced from the base of the plant and between the leaf axils on lower leaves. The flowers are borne in clusters, as many as ten per bunch. The sepals and petals are green, dotted with red-brown, and the pouched yellow lip is dotted maroon with white fringe. This plant grows well in a pot with fir bark.

NOTE: Although this plant prefers high humidity, it will do well at room conditions; always provide good drainage. A very suitable plant for an indoor windowsill garden.

GASTROCHILUS DASYPOGON

LIGHT: Bright
HUMIDITY: 60 percent
TEMPERATURE: 68–80°F.
FLOWERING: Variable

This plant has 5-inch-long deep green leaves. The brown flowers are borne between the leaf axils. The white lip has an orange blotch and tiny purple spots. Grow this orchid in a pot with fir bark.

NOTE: The leaves will spot if you leave water standing on them. Water the plant well two or three times weekly; do *not* spray leaves.

GASTROCHILUS SOMAI

LIGHT: BRIGHT
HUMIDITY: 50 percent
TEMPERATURE: 55–75°F.
FLOWERING: Summer

The flowers, produced in umbels, appear between the lower leaves. The sepals and petals are light green; the white ruffled lip has yellow and burgundy splotches dotted with brown. Grow the plant in a pot with fir bark.

NOTE: Provide good air circulation and ample drainage; mist the plant occasionally.

HARAELLA

From Taiwan, this is a genus of only one species, but what a tiny beauty it is. Leathery leaves in clusters are about 3 inches long and the flower, ½ inch across and ¾ inches long, is yellowish-white with oval sepals and petals at the top half of the flower and a fiddle-shaped fringed lip dotted with deep maroon.

Plants do best on a wooden slab and need daily spraying—best to keep in a well-ventilated and airy place.

HARAELLA ODORATA

LIGHT: Bright/Sun
HUMIDITY: 40 percent
TEMPERATURE: 60–75°F.
FLOWERING: Summer

This orchid has 1-inch green leathery leaves. The yellowish flowers have a maroon blotch on their lips; the blooms resemble a small insect. Grow the plant lashed to cork bark kept evenly moist.

NOTE: With bright light and even moisture, blooms readily indoors. Highly recommended.

HOLCOGLOSSUM

With only a few species, this genus of plants from Taiwan bears lovely white flowers that are rather large for the plant. The leaves are to 2 inches, needlelike, and few to a plant. In essence, the Holcoglossums without flowers are not much to look at, but in bloom they are handsome. Flowers are white and flat-faced with yellow on side lobes.

These dainty miniatures grow well on wood slabs and require good humidity; water the plants and then allow them to dry out before watering again. These are desirable plants because most of them bloom in winter.

HOLCOGLOSSUM QUASISPINIFOLIUM

LIGHT: Sun
HUMIDITY: 40 percent
TEMPERATURE: 55–75°F.
FLOWERING: Fall/Winter

The narrow leaves of this plant are 8 inches long and deep green. The flowers, somewhat large for the size of the plant, are white with a lip stained yellow. Grow the plant in a pot with fir bark. Keep the plant evenly moist all year.

NOTE: A very handsome and worthwhile indoor plant, not to be missed; no special requirements.

IONOPSIS

Ionopsis, from Peru, is easy to grow and popular. Leaves are usually needlelike, and the branching flower stems are long, from 6 to 7 inches, with many flowers. Flowers range in color from white to pink.

Ionopsis orchids are desirable where the growing area is cool—most do well at 50°F. Mount the plants on cork bark slabs and allow them to dry out between watering. Humidity is not vital. These are nice little orchids but not outstanding.

IONOPSIS UTRICULARIOIDES

LIGHT: Bright/Sun

HUMIDITY: 20 percent

TEMPERATURE: 50–80°F:

FLOWERING: Fall

The 1½- to 2½-inch medium green leaves are in pairs. The flowers are white to rose with purple markings; the lip has two lobes. Grow this orchid in a pot with fir bark.

NOTE: Likes moisture; a plant that is not spectacular but worthwhile.

KINGIELLA

Kingiella, sometimes classified as Doritis, is a genus of a few species. These splendid plants look like a Phalaenopsis and bear delicate shell-pink flowers. A healthy plant blooms over a long period of time, one flower following another. This orchid is generally undemanding and offers nice color.

KINGIELLA PHILIPPINENSIS

KINGIELLA PHILIPPINENSIS

LIGHT: Bright
HUMIDITY: 30 percent
TEMPERATURE: 60–80°F.
FLOWERING: Summer

The 6-inch-long leaves produce open-faced shell-pink flowers that are ¾ inch in diameter. Grow in pots with fir bark or on slabs.

NOTE: Keep plant somewhat dry for best results.

KINGIELLA TAENALIS

LIGHT: Bright
HUMIDITY: 40 percent
TEMPERATURE: 50–65°F.
FLOWERING: Fall

Long, dark green rhizomes produce 1- to 2-inch-long dark green leathery leaves; purple flowers are in clusters. Grow in a pot with fir bark or mounted on slabs.

NOTE: Plant can be grown somewhat dry.

KOELLENSTEINIA

With about ten species in the genus, Koellensteinias are generally epiphytic, ranging from Panama to the northern part of South America to Brazil. Some plants have small pseudobulbs; others form a clump of grasslike leaves. Flowers have a fleshy texture.

KOELLENSTEINIA GRAMINEA

LIGHT: Bright/Shade
HUMIDITY: 30 percent
TEMPERATURE: 55–75°F.
FLOWERING: Fall

This orchid's grassy foliage is about 8 inches long. The flowers, about 1 inch across, are yellow with purple bars; the lip is pale purple marked with yellow. The plant does well in pots with fir bark.

NOTE: Flowers last a long time—about six weeks on the plant. Can tolerate shade if necessary.

KOELLENSTEINIA TOLIMENSIS

LIGHT: Bright/Shade

HUMIDITY: 30 percent

TEMPERATURE: 55–75°F.

FLOWERING: Fall

This charming miniature is infrequently seen; it resembles *K. graminea.*

NOTE: Flowers last a long time; fine house plant.

Koellensteinia tolimensis

LAELIA

Laelia, closely allied to Cattleya, is a genus from South America with about seventy species. The majority require a place at a south window in direct sunlight, and even then these handsome plants may not bloom. Such sun-loving epiphytes are a challenge but certainly worthwhile.

Generally, these orchids carry one or two fleshy evergreen leaves. The flower spike is produced from the top of the pseudobulb; the pseudobulbs vary in size and shape. Several of the species are dwarf plants that produce brilliant yellow or orange flowers at various times of year. Others make extremely large plants, carrying spikes 6 feet long and crowded with spectacular bloom.

LAELIA FLAVA

LIGHT: Bright/Sun
HUMIDITY: 50 percent
TEMPERATURE: 60–80°F.
FLOWERING: January to June

This plant has one-leaved pseudobulbs. The small golden-yellow flowers have narrow sepals and petals with a ruffled lip. Grow the plant on an osmunda slab.

NOTE: This orchid likes warmth, humidity, and sunny conditions.

LAELIA LUNDII

LIGHT: Bright
HUMIDITY: 60 percent
TEMPERATURE: 60–75°F.
FLOWERING: Summer

The 1½-inch-long pseudobulbs usually have 6-inch-long 2-leaved green leaves. The 1½- to 2-inch lilac-rose flowers have narrow sepals and petals; the lip is tri-lobed. Grow the plant in a pot with chopped fir bark.

NOTE: Plant needs plenty of sun.

LAELIA PUMILA

LIGHT: Sun
HUMIDITY: 30 percent
TEMPERATURE: 55–75°F.
FLOWERING: Variable

Extremely pretty, *L. pumila* has 4-inch dark green leathery leaves and bears a rose-purple flower, large for the size of the plant. Grow in fir bark in a pot; keep evenly moist all year. Here is an orchid sure to please—you can depend on it to bloom. Don't miss it.

NOTE: Plant must have at least three hours of sun per day to bear flowers.

LAELIA PUMILA

LAELIA RUBESCENS

LIGHT: Bright

HUMIDITY: 50 percent

TEMPERATURE: 60–75°F.

FLOWERING: Fall

The leaves of this plant are 3 to 5 inches long, dark green, and leathery. There are small clusters of little lilac-mauve flowers borne on a wiry stem. The lip is lemon-white with a purple throat. Grow in fir bark in a pot.

NOTE: This orchid grows best in good humidity. It must have moving fresh air or the spikes and buds will mildew.

LEPTOTES

Native to Brazil and Paraguay, Leptotes is a genus of four species of attractive epiphytic orchids. Only a few species are listed in catalogues but Leptotes are becoming popular plants. In flowers, this is the biggest bargain imaginable from dwarf plants.

Grow Leptotes in small well-drained pots with tightly packed osmunda. Put plants in a bright spot. If you provide daytime warmth and cool evenings, you will have a splendid array of flowers in June, July, and August.

LEPTOTES BICOLOR

LIGHT: Sun
HUMIDITY: 20 percent
TEMPERATURE: 60–80°F.
FLOWERING: Summer

This plant has a solitary, pencil-like leaf 5 inches tall. The flower spike comes from the base of the leaf and is borne on a short stem. The pure white bloom is mammoth for the size of the plant—about 3 inches across—and the lip is stained magenta. This is a superlative orchid best grown in fir bark in a pot.

NOTE: Be sure plant has sufficient drainage; flowers last several weeks on the plant.

LYCASTE

Mostly epiphytic, Lycaste, a genus of about thirty species, includes handsome orchids from Mexico, Cuba, Peru, and Brazil, and these often respond better to window culture than greenhouse treatment. Plants are deciduous or semi-deciduous, and the long-lasting flowers vary greatly in size and color. Unlike some genera, the pseudobulbs of Lycaste produce several flower spikes; a plant can have as many as six to ten flowers.

The plants have fan-shaped clumps of leaves 2 to 3 feet tall. Flowers are usually carried on short, erect scapes from the base of the last-made pseudobulb, often after the leaves have shed and along with the young growth.

LYCASTE DEPEII

LIGHT: Bright

HUMIDITY: 40 percent

TEMPERATURE: 60–80°F.

FLOWERING: Summer

The 10-inch-long green leaves are produced from dark green pseudobulbs. The sepals are greenish-yellow with red spots, the petals are white, and the lip is white spotted red. Grow this orchid in a pot with fir bark.

NOTE: New plantlets appear at the base of older pseudobulbs and can be cut and grown separately.

MASDEVALLIA

Masdevallia is a fine genus of unusual orchids, a great many of them are a good size for the windowsill. The flowers are remarkable. The sepals usually extend into a long tail, earning the plants the name of Kite orchids. Found in Mexico, Bolivia, and Brazil, with the majority in the cloud forests of the Colombian Andes, these orchids do not have pseudobulbs. The leaves grow from a creeping rhizome. Some plants produce pendant flowers; in others, the flowers are on erect, tall scapes. The flowers can be small, about 1 inch long, or as long as 10 inches. The flowers are unusual not only in structure but in color, running the gamut from orange to almost black. Once very popular, Masdevallias are again appearing in choice collections. They are inexpensive and plentiful, and many species have successive blooms for many months.

This genus of plants prefers shade and high humidity—70 percent. You must keep the potting medium moderately moist at all times and provide good air circulation. Because they have no pseudobulbs and require constant moisture at the roots, Masdevallias must have a compost that drains readily. Masdevallias bloom off old flower stalks again and again, so do not cut the stems.

MASDEVALLIA BELLA

LIGHT: Bright/Shade
HUMIDITY: 40 percent
TEMPERATURE: 50–70°F.
FLOWERING: Fall

Ten inches tall, this orchid bears a pendant scape with large triangular flowers. The sepals are yellow, spotted red, with dark tails. Grow the plant in pots of fir bark.

NOTE: This plant likes it shady and moist; dry out slightly in late summer.

MASDEVALLIA CAUDATA

LIGHT: Shade/Bright
HUMIDITY: 30 percent
TEMPERATURE: 50–70°F.
FLOWERING: Variable

About 5 inches high, this orchid is always desirable. The upper sepals are yellow spotted and veined red; the lateral sepals are almost purple. Grow in a pot with fir bark.

NOTE: The plant is easy to grow; needs even moisture. Blooms on and off for several months.

MASDEVALLIA COCCINEA

LIGHT: Bright/Shade
HUMIDITY: 40 percent
TEMPERATURE: 45–65°F.
FLOWERING: Winter

This is a real beauty, with 7-inch-long, hard, textured green leaves; the red flowers are an inch long and on an arching spike that is kitelike. The inner throat is yellow. Grow in a pot with a mixture of chopped osmunda and perlite; keep evenly moist.

NOTE: Dry out slightly in fall to promote bloom. Not to be missed.

Masdevallia coccinea

MASDEVALLIA 'DORIS'

LIGHT: Bright
HUMIDITY: 40 percent
TEMPERATURE: 45–65°F.
FLOWERING: Fall

The ½-inch-long, elliptical, deep green leaves are produced on stalks, in clumps. The small, yellow flowers are kite-shaped. Grow in a pot with fir bark. Somewhat dry.

NOTE: Somewhat difficult to grow.

MASDEVALLIA HORRIDA

LIGHT: Shade/Bright
HUMIDITY: 30 percent
TEMPERATURE: 50–75°F.
FLOWERING: Variable

This plant has 2-inch-long leaves and tiny greenish-yellow triangular flowers dotted with red. It blooms for almost six months of the year. Grow in fir bark in a pot; keep evenly moist.

NOTE: No special requirements; easy to bloom; highly recommended.

MASDEVALLIA INFRACTA

LIGHT: Bright
HUMIDITY: 30 percent
TEMPERATURE: 50–75°F.
FLOWERING: Variable

With 6-inch leathery leaves, *M. infracta* bears dozens of whitish "tailed" flowers marked purple—most unusual. Plants do best in fir bark in pots but can also be grown on slabs. Keep the plants quite moist in warm weather—dry out a little in cold months.

NOTE: No special requirements.

Masdevallia infracta (PHOTO BY JOYCE WILSON)

MASDEVALLIA PERISTERIA

LIGHT: Bright
HUMIDITY: 30 percent
TEMPERATURE: 50–70°F.
FLOWERING: Variable

This orchid, known for its large fleshy flowers, had dark green foliage; the flowers are green marked with purple spots. The long tails are greenish-yellow. Grow the plant in fir bark in a pot; keep evenly moist all year. This one is unusual and worth a try.

NOTE: No special requirements.

MASDEVALLIA PERISTERIA

MASDEVALLIA SCHLIMII

LIGHT: Bright
HUMIDITY: 40 percent
TEMPERATURE: 45–65°F.
FLOWERING: Variable

This plant has 2- to 4-inch-long light green leaves on a 3-inch stalk. The flowers are small, dotted red. Grow the plant in a pot with a mixture of chopped osmunda, fir bark, and perlite kept evenly moist.

NOTE: Fine miniature; blooms for months.

MASDEVALLIA SCHROEDERIANA

LIGHT: Bright
HUMIDITY: 30 percent
TEMPERATURE: 55–75°F.
FLOWERING: Summer/Fall

This orchid bears large purple flowers with long yellow tails. The leaves are grassy, 2 to 4 inches long. Grow in fir bark in a pot.

NOTE: Keep evenly moist; will tolerate more light than most Masdevallias.

MASDEVALLIA TOVARENSIS

LIGHT: Bright
HUMIDITY: 40 percent
TEMPERATURE: 45–65°F.
FLOWERING: Fall/Winter

The 3- to 4-inch-long glossy light green leaves are produced in clumps. The kite-shaped white flowers appear on graceful stems. Grow this plant in a pot with a mixture of chopped osmunda and fir bark.

NOTE: Dry out the plant somewhat in late summer to promote blooms. Easy to grow at windows.

MASDEVALLIA TRIANGULARIS

LIGHT: Bright
HUMIDITY: 30 percent
TEMPERATURE: 55–75°F.
FLOWERING: Winter

Eight-inch-long leaves and yellow flowers that are dotted purple characterize this plant. This is a most unusual orchid, and it flowers in the winter. Grow in fir bark in a pot.

NOTE: Keep evenly moist; no other special requirements.

MAXILLARIA

With over 300 species, Maxillarias from Mexico and Central and South America offer some fine small plants for indoor growing. Some have tufted leaves, and others are large and rambling. Flowers are yellow, red, or red-brown—sometimes plain, sometimes spotted with darker colors. Plants are prone to bloom in summer but there are also some species that bear winter flowers; some even bloom on and off throughout the year. Plants are best grown in pots of fir bark; place in bright light and provide even moisture all year. Maxillarias generally are amenable plants that do well indoors.

Maxillaria (unidentified)

MAXILLARIA COBANENSIS

LIGHT: Bright
HUMIDITY: 30 percent
TEMPERATURE: 55–75°F.
FLOWERING: Summer

The plant has slender pseudobulbs and single leaves about 4 inches long. The flowers are tan with dark red spots or lines and a scoop-shaped lip. Grow in fir bark in a pot; keep moderately moist all year. Give the plant bright light.

NOTE: Plant needs good light and even moisture all year; otherwise, no special requirements.

MAXILLARIA TENUIFOLIA

LIGHT: Bright
HUMIDITY: 40 percent
TEMPERATURE: 55–75°F.
FLOWERING: Spring/Summer

This is a leafy green plant with foliage about 3 inches long and handsome dark red flowers mottled white. Grow it in small pots with fir bark; keep moderately moist—do not overwater.

NOTE: Almost grows by itself—and can be depended upon to bloom; highly recommended.

Maxillaria tenuifolia

MAXILLARIA VARIABILIS

LIGHT: Bright
HUMIDITY: 30 percent
TEMPERATURE: 55–75°F.
FLOWERING: Variable

A very popular species, this plant has dark green curving leaves and cylindrical pseudobulbs. Flowers are yellow or red on short stems, and a healthy plant has many blooms. Grow in fir bark in a pot and give even moisture all year. Very easy to grow and floriferous.

NOTE: No special requirements.

MICROCOELIA

Orchids are versatile plants, and this genus of leafless species proves the point. The plants are clumps of roots that form a compound, and sprays of minute white flowers come from the twigs. From Kenya, Uganda, West Africa, and Tanzania, these are oddities but always interesting. Flowers usually appear in summer or fall and, generally, plants are easily grown on small branches. They need good light and frequent misting.

MICROCOELIA EXILIS

LIGHT: Bright
HUMIDITY: 60 percent
TEMPERATURE: 50–70°F.
FLOWERING: Fall

With branching roots and stems, these plants bear minute flowers in abundance—they are white with broad sepals and petals. Grow the plant on a small branch and mist daily. Bizarre but beautiful.

NOTE: Plant must be misted daily and kept in an area with exceptionally good air circulation.

MICROCOELIA GUYONIANA

LIGHT: Bright
HUMIDITY: 60 percent
TEMPERATURE: 50–70°F.
FLOWERING: Summer

Probably the most popular in the genus, this species has rather thick branching roots and bears a pendulous flower spike loaded with white, somewhat large flowers (about ½ inch long). The blossoms open all at one time—usually in summer. Grow on a small branch and mist daily. Very pretty.

NOTE: Keep plant in an area with good air circulation.

MILTONIA

Miltonia is a handsome genus of large-flowered epiphytes distributed through Costa Rica and Brazil, with a great many from the Andes. The genus is divided into cool-growing and warm-growing varieties. However, even the heat-tolerant kinds need careful handling in order to survive a very hot summer. Plants require more time and care than most orchids but the perfectly arranged bouquets of pansylike bloom are worth considerable effort.

Mainly small plants, the Miltonias have elongated pseudobulbs tipped with several light green leaves. Even when out of bloom the plants are attractive. The flower spike is produced from the cont.

base of the most recently formed pseudobulb and is erect, or sometimes arching, and carries either a solitary flower or many flowers.
The inflorescence of the cool-growers is white or pink blotched
with crimson or magenta. The warm-growers produce star-shaped
yellow or white flowers marked purple or brown. There are many
highly-colored hybrids available now.

MILTONIA ROEZLII

LIGHT: Bright
HUMIDITY: 55 percent
TEMPERATURES: 55–75°F.
FLOWERING: Spring/Summer

A plant that can grow to twelve inches, with light green, grasslike
leaves, *M. Roezlii* produces flowers about five per stalk and 1¼
inches across. The sepals are pure white, the petals have a purple
eye, and the large, flat, white lip has a yellow eye. Grow this orchid
in a pot with fir bark.

NOTE: New plants appear in May between old bulbs. Grows well
on a windowsill.

MYSTACIDIUM

These are tiny orchids from Africa, and what beautiful plants they are. They are short-stemmed with a few leaves; the flowers are most often white but a few are greenish or yellowish. Plants produce many flowers in a somewhat clustered arrangement. There are species for all blooming seasons of the year.

Grow Mystacidiums on cork bark and keep plants well-moistened. Give the plant bright light but no sun. This genus is a very pretty addition to the collection and easy to grow.

MYSTACIDIUM CAPENSE

LIGHT: Bright
HUMIDITY: 40 percent
TEMPERATURE: 60–80°F.
FLOWERING: Summer

This plant has 2-inch leathery leaves; the flowers grow to ½ inch across in clusters and are usually white with greenish markings. Grow in a pot with fir bark or on slabs.

NOTE: These plants need warmth and strong light. Keep evenly moist at all times. Generally easy to grow.

Oncidium

Oncidium is a large and varied genus of more than 700 epiphytic orchids distributed throughout Central America, Mexico, the West Indies, and parts of Brazil. Generally called Spray orchids, the majority produce long spikes of beautiful yellow flowers marked with brown; they are welcome additions to any window collection.

Many plants in the genus have compressed pseudobulbs tipped by one or two fleshy leaves; others are almost without pseudobulbs; and still others have pencil-like leaves. All are evergreen. The flower spike is generally produced from the base of the pseudobulb and in most cases is flexible and arching. Flowers are small and numerous or large and few, depending on the species. A great many species of this genus bloom in autumn or winter and the flowers last a long time on the plant, often seven or nine weeks.

ONCIDIUM BAHAMENSE

LIGHT: Bright
HUMIDITY: 40 percent
TEMPERATURE: 62–75°F.
FLOWERING: Summer

This orchid has 2- to 3-inch-long green, needlelike leaves folded with toothed edges, and dainty yellow flowers. Grow the plant in a pot with chopped osmunda and fir bark.

NOTE: Plant needs good moisture and bright light to bloom.

ONCIDIUM DESERTORUM

LIGHT: Bright/Sun
HUMIDITY: 40 percent
TEMPERATURE: 62–75°F.
FLOWERING: Fall

This epiphyte has no pseudobulbs. The dark green leaves are 2 to 3 inches long, folded, and small-toothed, with tiny red brown specks. The flowers are borne on long, thin, canelike scapes that grow up to 20 inches tall on some plants. There are many flowers to a cluster. The bright yellow petals have darker, brownish markings closer to their centers. Grow in a pot with fir bark kept evenly moist.

NOTE: Grow these orchids in a bright window.

Oncidium desertorum

ONCIDIUM LEIBOLDII

LIGHT: Bright
HUMIDITY: 40 percent
TEMPERATURE: 62–75°F.
FLOWERING: Variable

This epiphyte has 1- to 2-inch-long folded green leaves. Long, thin, canelike spikes appear between leaf axils and produce many small white flowers that have reddish splotches and a yellow center. Grow this orchid in a pot with fir bark; keep somewhat dry.

NOTE: This is a great plant for a beginner because it is easy to care for, needing only occasional watering. The flowers bloom twice a year and last for a long time.

ONCIDIUM MACROPETALUM

LIGHT: Bright
HUMIDITY: 60 percent
TEMPERATURE: 60–75°F.
FLOWERING: Winter

These orchids have swollen pseudobulbs, with one light green, 2-inch-long leaf. The bright yellow flowers have brown spots, and the petals are flat. Grow in fir bark in a pot; keep quite moist.

NOTE: Plant needs warmth and humid conditions and is difficult but worth a try.

ORNITHOCEPHALUS

With thirty-five species, Ornithocephalus are all small epiphytes from Mexico to Trinidad to Brazil. They have fleshy foliage arranged in tight clumps and bear small green or white blossoms, usually in late fall.

Grow these orchids in osmunda, and keep them wet at all times. They will bloom in shade or in the sun and generally need minimum nighttime temperatures of about 60°F. Although not showy, the plants hold their flowers for many months and are good for the home or greenhouse.

Ornithocephalus grandiflorum (PHOTO BY JOYCE WILSON)

ORNITHOCEPHALUS GRANDIFLORUM

ORNITHOCEPHALUS GRANDIFLORUM

LIGHT: Bright
HUMIDITY: 40 percent
TEMPERATURE: 60–75°F.
FLOWERING: Summer/Fall

This is an unusual little plant, with furry, rhizomelike runners. The 2-inch-long light green leaves are produced from a narrow bulb. The leaves and bulbs grow in a fan shape. The ¼-inch flowers are creamy white, with a birdlike appearance. Grow this orchid in a pot with fir bark.

NOTE: This plant grows well with good air circulation.

ORNITHOCHILUS

Ornithochilus is a small genus of epiphytic orchids allied with Aerides. The leaves are usually about 9 inches long, and plants bear curiously shaped red and yellow flowers, several to a pendant scape; they bloom in summer and sometimes again in winter.

The plants need warmth, humidity, and bright light and so are best for greenhouse growing. They do best on pieces of tree fern kept saturated with water.

ORNITHOCHILUS FUSCUS

LIGHT: Bright

HUMIDITY: 20 percent

TEMPERATURE: 55–75°F.

FLOWERING: Winter

The arching spikes of flowers are ½ inch across; the leaves are dark green. The sepals and petals are yellow, streaked with red, and the spurred lip is handsomely bearded. Grow the plant on slabs; dry out somewhat between waterings.

NOTE: Dry out to encourage bloom; easy to grow indoors.

PHALAENOPSIS

Phalaenopsis, a genus of about seventy species of beautiful orchids from Java, Sumatra, Asia, and the Philippines, is commonly known as the Dogwood orchid—the flowers resemble dogwood. The white flowers are popular for corsages and for cutting. The botanicals are smaller and bear fewer flowers.

The genus is characterized by absence of pseudobulbs; the plants have short stems bearing three or more leathery leaves. The roots are mostly flat, often long, winding in and around the pot and reaching into the air for moisture. Flower spikes are produced from leaf axils and are single or branched, short or extremely long.

Phalaenopsis cornu cervi

PHALAENOPSIS CORNU CERVI

LIGHT: Bright
HUMIDITY: 45 percent
TEMPERATURE: 60–75°F.
FLOWERING: Summer

This delightful bulbless species has 6- to 10-inch-long glossy, light green leaves. The ascending stalk bears 2-inch flowers; the petals and sepals are yellowish-green spotted with red-brown, and the whitish lip is clawed. Grow this orchid in a pot with fir bark.

NOTE: Water two to three times weekly; not very tolerant of cold temperatures.

PHALAENOPSIS PARISHII

LIGHT: Bright
HUMIDITY: 40 percent
TEMPERATURE: 75°F.
FLOWERING: Summer

This orchid has ¾-inch glossy deep green leaves. The 1-inch flowers are borne on short stems and the sepals and petals are white; the petals have two brown bands. Grow in a pot with fir bark; keep evenly moist.

NOTE: This easy-to-grow plant needs good air circulation.

PHYSOSIPHON

From the Pleurothallis group we have Physosiphon, with only a few species. The plants have single leaves and bear a flowering stem that is loaded with small greenish-white tubular flowers that make a handsome display in spring or summer. These miniatures need bright, airy conditions and good humidity; otherwise they take care of themselves. This is a pleasing, though unspectacular, plant.

PHYSOSIPHON PUBESCENS

LIGHT: Bright
HUMIDITY: 40 percent
TEMPERATURE: 55–80°F.
FLOWERING: Spring

Here is a tiny creeping plant that spreads matlike; it has fleshy leaves and paired flowers hidden among the leaves. The flowers are usually white. Best grown on cork slabs, *P. pubescens* is difficult to cultivate in pots. Give the plants bright light and keep them evenly moist all year.

NOTE: Plant needs a bright airy place to bloom.

PHYSOSIPHON TUBATUS

LIGHT: Bright
HUMIDITY: 40 percent
TEMPERATURE: 55–75°F.
FLOWERING: Summer

This plant grows into a dense cluster of rather large leaves (to 14 inches); the flowers are abundant, usually greenish-white, sometimes tinged orange. The plant needs a bright, airy place and moisture. Grow *P. tubatus* in a pot with fir bark; keep moist.

NOTE: Mist plant daily; give bright, buoyant atmosphere.

PLEIONE

Pleione is a genus of about twenty species of mainly small terrestrial bulbous-type orchids from China and Southeast Asia. They are sometimes called Indian crocus. Large showy solitary flowers appear on 3- to 4-inch plants. Most species bear autumn flowers that last a week to ten days on the plant. Pleiones thrive in bright light (no sun) and should be potted in equal parts leaf mold, sand, and fine-grade fir bark.

When bulbs are first potted, water this genus carefully. They are tricky in this respect and too much water can kill plants if roots are not expanded. The plants are deciduous. After the leaves fall, water scantily; a definite rest period of say, six to eight weeks is imperative for Pleiones. They are temperamental beauties.

PLEIONE HOOKERIANA

LIGHT: Bright/Shade
HUMIDITY: 30 percent
TEMPERATURE: 55–75°F.
FLOWERING: Fall/Winter

With foliage about 5 inches high, *P. hookeriana* bears leaves and flowers at the same time. They are rose colored, almost purple, with a brown splotch on the lip. The plant produces solitary flowers, but a healthy one may have several blooms. Grow in equal parts fir bark and soil. Do not overwater.

NOTE: Remember to observe rest time, or plants will not bloom.

PLEIONE LAGENARIA

PLEIONE LAGENARIA

LIGHT: Bright
HUMIDITY: 30 percent
TEMPERATURE: 50–75°F.
FLOWERING: Winter

With angular pseudobulbs and pale thin green leaves, this orchid bears large, handsome, rose-lilac flowers. Grow the plant in equal parts soil and fir bark in pots. Water judiciously—too much moisture can cause rot. After the plant has bloomed, rest it for several weeks. *P. lagenaria* is an outstanding plant.

NOTE: Observe natural rest time.

PLEIONE PRICEI

LIGHT: Bright
HUMIDITY: 30 percent
TEMPERATURE: 55–75°F.
FLOWERING: Winter

This orchid has leaves about 6 inches high and flowers almost 5 inches across, pale rose with a white fringed lip. Grow in pots with equal parts fir bark and soil; do not overwater.

NOTE: Plants need a definite rest period—leave almost dry for about six weeks.

PLEUROTHALLIS

Pleurothallis is a genus of more than 500 species growing through southern Florida, Mexico, and Brazil. Generally miniatures, they are easy to grow, and they bloom continually through the warm months. Some of these epiphytes carry a solitary leaf, others have tufted growth, and a few have leaves spaced on a creeping rhizome.

The small flowers are pretty, although in many cases a magnifying glass is needed to truly appreciate their beauty. Pleurothallis should be grown with bright light (some sun) in moderate temperatures—60°F. at night—and the potting mixture—fir bark or osmunda—should never become completely dry. These inexpensive plants thrive in the home or greenhouse.

PLEUROTHALLIS ARIBULOIDES

LIGHT: Bright
HUMIDITY: 50 percent
TEMPERATURE: 60–75°F.
FLOWERING: Fall/Spring

This orchid has 1- to 2-inch-long semiglossy, elliptic, green leaves. The many orange-red flowers appear at the base of the leaves. Grow the plant in a pot with fir bark, or on a slab of cork bark kept moist.

NOTE: Plant likes warm and humid conditions; always provide sufficient air circulation.

PLEUROTHALLIS CHRYSANTHA

LIGHT: Bright
HUMIDITY: 40 percent
TEMPERATURE: 55–75°F.
FLOWERING: Variable

About 6 inches high, this orchid is radiant with a mass of tiny burnt orange flowers at the base of the leaves. The blooms appear on and off all summer. Grow mounted on a moist slab.

NOTE: Keep plant evenly moist.

PLEUROTHALLIS GROBYI

LIGHT: Sun/Bright
HUMIDITY: 50 percent
TEMPERATURE: 62–75°F.
FLOWERING: Fall

P. grobyi has light green flowers with burgundy stripes on a wiry arching stalk. The translucent light-yellow lower sepals grow together and then separate into an inset lip and the petals. Grow on cork bark or in a small pot with fir bark; keep evenly moist.

NOTE: Easy to grow; no special requirements.

PLEUROTHALLIS IMMERSA

LIGHT: Bright
HUMIDITY: 40 percent
TEMPERATURE: 55–75°F.
FLOWERING: Variable

This miniature, larger than usual, has succulent, glossy leaves and a long scape of vivid orange, long-lasting flowers. The unusual flower spike emerges from a point near the tip of the leaves. Grow in fir bark in a pot; keep evenly moist.

NOTE: Flowers appear on and off for several months.

PLEUROTHALLIS LONGISSIMA

LIGHT: Bright
HUMIDITY: 40 percent
TEMPERATURE: 60–80°F.
FLOWERING: Summer

This 9-inch plant has erect scapes of whitish-yellow flowers. Not as handsome as the other orchids listed here, it is easy to cultivate. Grow in fir bark in a pot; keep evenly moist.

NOTE: *P. longissima* is a floriferous plant; easy to grow.

PLEUROTHALLIS PLATYSEMOS

LIGHT: Bright
HUMIDITY: 55 percent
TEMPERATURE: 62–75°F.
FLOWERING: Winter

With fibrous roots and thin, needlelike stems, each with a 1¼-inch-long succulent dark green leaf with purple specks P. *platyslemos* bears 6 to 8 flowers on a pendant scape; the sepals are light green and transparent, and petals have a darker green lip. Grow in fir bark in a pot; keep evenly moist.

NOTE: Mist occasionally and water two to three times weekly. The pot must have good drainage.

Pleurothallis platysemos

PLEUROTHALLIS RESUPINATA

LIGHT: Bright
HUMIDITY: 40 percent
TEMPERATURE: 65–80°F.
FLOWERING: Fall

An orchid with 2-inch-long dull green leaves spotted deep purple on their undersides, *P. resupinata* has beige flowers, spotted with maroon. Grow in a pot with fir bark kept somewhat dry.

NOTE: *P. resupinata* likes more warmth than most Pleurothallis.

PLEUROTHALLIS TELETIFOLIUM

LIGHT: Bright/Sun
HUMIDITY: 40 percent
TEMPERATURE: 60–75°F.
FLOWERING): SUMMER/FALL

The orchid, with ⅜- to ½-inch-long slender stalks, each with one ½-inch-long green leaf, has as many as ten flowers per leaf. The sepals are transparent and green, and the petals have a flattened lip spotted with deep burgundy. Grow in a pot with fir bark kept somewhat dry.

NOTE: Water the plant once a week; provide good drainage.

PLEUROTHALLIS TRIDENTATA

LIGHT: Bright

HUMIDITY: 30 percent

TEMPERATURE: 55–75°F.

FLOWERING: Variable

A very attractive pot plant whether in bloom or not, *P. tridentata* has heart-shaped leaves and tiny yellow-green flowers nestled at the base of each leaf. Grow in small pots of fir bark kept evenly moist all year.

NOTE: Plant blooms on and off throughout the year.

Pleurothallis tridentata

POLYSTACHYA

Polystachya is a genus widely distributed throughout Africa, Asia and America, the greater number of the 100 known species being small or miniature plants. The tiny, cup-shaped flowers appear in a wide range of colors, usually in the summer months. *Polystachya luteola* and *P. pubescens* are most commonly seen.

These epiphytes have short stems basally sheathed with leaves. Often, the stems thicken to form small pseudobulbs that are tipped with two or three leaves. The flower spike, arching or erect, is produced from the apex of the bulbs.

POLYSTACHYA LUTEOLA

LIGHT: Bright/Sun
HUMIDITY: 30 percent
TEMPERATURE: 55–75°F.
FLOWERING: Summer

Handsome even without flowers, *P. luteola* has green, grasslike leaves; flower spikes are produced at the base of the pseudobulbs and carry pendant stems of tiny yellow flowers that are shaded green and scented. Grow the plant on slabs or in pots with fir bark kept evenly moist all year. This orchid is pretty, and you can depend on it to bloom.

NOTE: Easily grown.

POLYSTACHYA LUTEOLA

POLYSTACHYA OTTONIANA

LIGHT: Sun
HUMIDITY: 30 percent
TEMPERATURE: 65–75°F.
FLOWERING: Variable

This orchid has three pair of 4-inch-long grasslike leaves. The white flowers have bright yellow stripes on their lips. Grow the plant in a pot with fir bark; keep somewhat dry.

NOTE: Give sun and warmth; otherwise easy to grow.

RESTREPIA

Little known but lovely, Restrepia is a genus of orchids mainly from Venezuela. They are now available, and are fascinating plants to grow. Restrepias, often included with the genus Pleurothallis, differ from that group in their number of pollinia and have larger and more handsome flowers.

Restrepias do best in coolness—50°F. at night—with some afternoon sunshine. Pot them in osmunda or fir bark, and keep them moist all year.

RESTREPIA ANTENNIFERA

LIGHT: Bright
HUMIDITY: 30 percent
TEMPERATURE: 50–70°F.
FLOWERING: Fall

This charming little plant has a single leathery green leaf. The yellow flowers are dotted red; the lower sepals have purple stripes. The handsome feature of the bloom is the two lateral sepals that are joined to form a single spoon-shaped pseudolip. Grow mounted on a moist slab.

NOTE: Plant likes it cool; dry out somewhat in late summer.

RESTREPIA ELEGANS

LIGHT: Bright
HUMIDITY: 30 percent
TEMPERATURE: 55–75°F.
FLOWERING: Summer

This plant resembles *R. antennifera* but is somewhat smaller.

NOTE: Grow the same as *R. antennifera*.

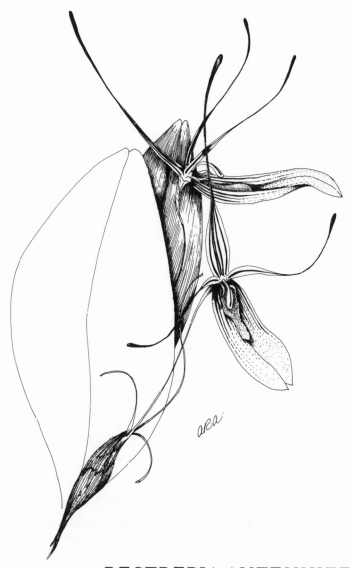

RESTREPIA ANTENNIFERA

SARCOCHILUS

Sarcochilus is a genus of epiphytic orchids from Burma, Australia, and the Philippines. The small flowers are a lovely rose-pink or blush-pink.

These orchids need warmth and must never be allowed to dry out completely. Grow them in tree fern fiber or on blocks of wood in a sunny spot. Warmth is best for these miniatures, but they also will tolerate a few nights of coolness.

SARCOCHILUS LUNIFERUS

LIGHT: Sun
HUMIDITY: 30 percent
TEMPERATURE: 65–75°F.
FLOWERING: Variable

This is a unique orchid because it has no true leaves. It does have a network of long roots and bears a drooping scape of lovely cupped yellow flowers dotted red. Give the plant a very slight rest with somewhat less water after flowering. Grow mounted on a moist slab.

NOTE: Keep warm and in the sun; very unusual.

SARCOCHILUS SEGAWII

LIGHT: Bright
HUMIDITY: 30 percent
TEMPERATURE: 60–80°F.
FLOWERING: Variable

This is a popular leafless orchid with thick roots; the flower stem is about 3 inches long with attractive, pale green, round flowers. Grow it on a slab of wood or bark; keep evenly moist all year. The plant is an oddity; very pretty.

NOTE: Plant likes even moisture at all times.

Sarcochilus segawii (PHOTO BY JOYCE WILSON)

SCHLIMIA

This small genus of epiphytic orchids from Colombia is hard to find but worth the search. Only one species is available, and it bears flowers that are large for the size of the plant.

Indicative of their mountain heritage, Schlimias need very cool temperatures—50°F. at night—and moist growing conditions. Although they will grow in pots of osmunda, the plants do better on a tree fern block. This orchid is for greenhouse growing only.

SCHLIMIA TRIFIDA

LIGHT: Bright
HUMIDITY: 30 percent
TEMPERATURE: 50–75°F.
FLOWERING: Summer

One inch tall, with 8-inch-long leaves S. *trifida* has a pendant stalk that bears fragrant white flowers spotted with purple and a white lip dramatically marked orange. Grow in fir bark in a pot; keep moist.

NOTE: Plant like it cool; keep quite moist.

SIGMATOSTALIX

Related to Oncidiums, this genus has several interesting plants. Most have pencil-like, grassy leaves or solitary, papery, thin (2- to 4-inch) leaves. Flowers are usually produced on long stems—many flowers to a stem—and have a long column with an enlarged lip. Plants do well in small clay pots; keep fir bark uniformly moist at all times. No rest periods are needed. These plants make nice additions to a collection.

SIGMATOSTALIX RADICANS

LIGHT: Bright
HUMIDITY: 20 percent
TEMPERATURE: 55–75°F.
FLOWERING: Summer

With three to five 5-inch-long, light green, narrow, grasslike leaves. *S. radicans* bears flowers 6 inches long. The sepals are light green to transparent, and the petals have a wide dark reddish lip and a yellow dot above the lip. Grow in a pot with fir bark; keep evenly moist.

NOTE: Provide good drainage and adequate humidity.

SOPHRONITIS

True miniatures, only 2 to 3 inches tall, Sophronitis is a difficult genus of orchids to cultivate indoors. However, the flowers are so exquisite—brilliant red—that they are worth your time.

Give these plants good light (but no sun) and try to keep them as cool as possible at all times. Heat quickly dessicates plants. Pot in fir bark and water liberally most of the year.

SOPHRONITIS GRANDIFLORA

LIGHT: Bright
HUMIDITY: 30 percent
TEMPERATURE: 45–75°F.
FLOWERING: Winter

A charmer, *S. grandiflora* has 2- to 3-inch dark green leathery leaves; the flowers are brilliant red, about 2 inches across. Grow in a pot with fir bark; keep quite moist.

NOTE: Keep plant in a cool, airy place.

STELIS

Stelis, a genus compared mainly of miniatures, includes about 500 species from tropical America, with a few from Brazil and Peru. They have a compound of small leaves, each leaf bearing a tall slender flower stem covered with blooms that look very much like beads on a string. Although not as easy to grow as other miniatures, once established Stelis plants bloom profusely.

STELIS GUATEMALENIS

LIGHT: Bright/Sun
HUMIDITY: 30 percent
TEMPERATURE: 60–80°F.
FLOWERING: Summer

This plant grows to 8 inches high. The extremely handsome greenish-white flowers are only ⅛ inch in diameter but shaped like a tulip. Grow in a pot with fir bark kept somewhat dry.

NOTE: Keep plant somewhat dry; can be depended upon to bloom indoors.

STELIS HYMENTHA

LIGHT: Bright/Sun
HUMIDITY: 30 percent
TEMPERATURE: 60–80°F.
FLOWERING: Summer

This orchid is not as attractive as S. *guatemalenis*. It grows to about 6 inches high and bears white flowers. Grow in a pot with fir bark kept somewhat dry.

NOTE: Plant can be depended upon to bloom indoors.

STELIS RUPRICHTIANA

LIGHT: Bright
HUMIDITY: 40 percent
TEMPERATURE: 62–75°F.
FLOWERING: Spring

With 1- to 2-inch-long glossy green leaves S. *ruprichtiana* bears flowers on 1½-inch-long spikes; ⅛-inch light green flowers with a deep burgundy center, 10 to 20 per spike, appear alongside the leaf. Grow in a clay pot with fir bark; keep evenly moist.

NOTE: Water several times weekly, and mist during the day.

STENOGLOTTIS

These are unusual orchids because after flowering the plants die down completely; new growth starts in about four months. They need a terrestrial potting mixture; use equal parts of soil and fine-grade fir bark. The foliage is papery thin, tending to grow in a circular cluster at the base of the plant, and hardly resembles that of an orchid. Flowers, usually pink, appear on a tall, mostly erect, stem—many flowers to a stem.

Keep potting mixture uniformly moist except when the plant is resting—then carry almost completely dry. Resume watering when you see new growth starting. Highly recommended.

STENOGLOTTIS LONGIFOLIA

LIGHT: Bright
HUMIDITY: 20 percent
TEMPERATURE: 55–75°F.
FLOWERING: Late summer or early fall

You can depend upon S. *longifolia* to bloom year after year. The leaves grow in a circular cluster; foliage is about 3 inches long. The long flower spikes—to 10 inches—bear dozens of very pretty pink flowers; dry out between waterings.

NOTE: Allow plant to dry out after blooming.

Stenoglottis longifolia
(PHOTO BY JOYCE WILSON)

Telipogon (unidentified) (PHOTO BY PAUL HUTCHINSON)

TELIPOGON

Telipogon is a genus of high-altitude (8,000 to 9,000 feet) orchids from Costa Rica, Brazil, and Peru. One species is available, and although it is difficult to cultivate, with a little care and a lot of luck you might get it to bloom. Certainly the beauty of the flower is worth the patience necessary to grow this plant.

This orchid requires very cool conditions. It does not want much sun and prefers a very moist but airy location.

TELIPOGON ANGUSTIFOLIA

LIGHT: Bright
HUMIDITY: 30 percent
TEMPERATURE: 45–75°F.
FLOWERING: Fall/Winter

T. angustifolia produces a yellow triangular flower; about 1 inch across, it is veined with brownish-yellow and white at its center, with a dull purple spot. This is a real beauty. Grow the plant mounted on moist slabs.

NOTE: Plant likes coolness and moisture; provide good humidity.

THRIXSPERMUM

Some of these orchids come from Brazil, others from Taiwan and the Philippines. The leaves are dark green, about 2 to 3 inches long in a somewhat clustered pattern. The plants bear lovely little white flowers with a pink spot on the lip. This group's asset is that most of its species bloom on and off throughout the year. Most require a somewhat damp and bright place to grow and should be watered copiously all year.

THRIXSPERMUM FORMOSANUM

LIGHT: Sun/Bright
HUMIDITY: 40 percent
TEMPERATURE: 62–75°F.
FLOWERING: Spring/Fall

This orchid has 2- to 3-inch-long dull green leaves. Small (¼-inch) pearl white flowers with faded purple tones on the back sides of the sepals and petals are produced on 2-inch spikes. The deep white lip has small, orange-brown, eyelike spots on each side of the lip and purple veins on the lower part of the lip, making the plant look like an insect. Grow in a small clay pot with fir bark; keep moist.

NOTE: The flowers open for about 12 hours and then close up and drop off. In about 2 days another flower opens; this cycle is repeated for 3 to 4 months. Some of these orchids may flower in the spring as well as the fall.

TRICHOCENTRUM

Related to Oncidiums, Trichocentrum are single-leaved plants with beautiful small flowers, generally white marked with pink or rose. Many species bloom in fall and winter, making them exceptionally valuable in collections. As a rule plants are easy to grow and need little more than moisture and bright light. A healthy plant produces many single-stemmed flowers. These are excellent plants for beginners.

TRICHOCENTRUM PFAVII

LIGHT: Bright/Shade
HUMIDITY: 20 percent
TEMPERATURE: 60–80°F.
FLOWERING: Winter

T. pfavii has 3-inch-long glossy green leaves; the flower spikes appear at the base of the plant. The flowers have a white ruffled lip that gleams and sparkles in the sunlight; there are red markings on the throat, sepal, and petals. Grow in a clay pot with fir bark; keep evenly moist.

NOTE: Very tolerant of low light and low humidity.

SIX

Other Miniature Orchids

This ends our study of the fine miniature orchids for home and greenhouse. Certainly we have not included all of the diminutive gems of the Orchidaceae—there are hundreds more. We have concentrated on the plants we have grown and/or known, and we hope that you take as much pleasure in growing these plants as we do.

In this last chapter, we discuss briefly a number of miniatures that are difficult to find now. In time they will be available to everyone. Because we did not grow every plant that follows, there are no specific cultural instructions; rather, we have given general directions collected from friends and growers who do cultivate the plants. Following each general description, we recommend two or more species.

Barbosella

A genus of pretty orchids from the cool cloud forests of South America, these plants need shade and even moisture all year. They are best grown on slabs or in small pots of fir bark. Barbosellas have small flowers—about ¼ inch—usually rose colored, occasionally greenish. The plants bear a resemblance to Restrepias. They are very pretty at a windowsill.

B. australis
B. cucullata

Cadetia

From New Guinea, these orchids are highly desirable because the flowers are large for the size of the plant and beautifully textured—almost crystalline. Plants need shade and warmth; grow in fir bark. A healthy specimen will bloom on and off throughout the year.

C. chamaephyton
C. dischorensis

Jumella

Mainly from Malagasy, these orchids, which resemble Angraecums, have lovely white or yellow fragrant flowers and straplike dark green leaves. Plants need to be grown in small pots of fine-grade fir bark, but you may also succeed using slabs. Keep these orchids somewhat moist; protect them from strong sunlight. These are amenable plants—generally, very easy to grow.

J. confusa
J. henyri

LANKESTERELLA

From Costa Rica, Venezuela, and Brazil these orchids are easy to grow, generally epiphytic, and have clusters of soft, tender leaves; flower spikes come from the center of the plant; the flowers are greenish-white. Provide constant moisture for the growing medium—usually fine-grade fir bark or slabs are used.

L. ceracifolia
L. orthnantha

NOTYLIA

From Central America, the Notylias offer a variety of plants—some have pseudobulbs, others a fan of leaves. Flowers are borne on slender spikes, many to a stalk. They are feathery in appearance, usually white or green, sometimes lilac. Plants need bright light; keep them moist all year. They grow well in small pots of fir bark or on slabs.

N. bicolor
N. xyphorius

A fine specimen of *Notylia xyphorius*

PROMENAEA

A group of small orchids from Brazil, these plants are related to Zygopetalums and have rounded, compressed pseudobulbs and pairs of leaves. Foliage is light green and soft; the flowers exquisite in tones of yellow with maroon spots. Flowers are large for the size of the plant. These miniatures need a somewhat shady location; water sparingly—too much moisture can cause rot. Promenaeas are nice charmers for windows.

P. stapelioides
P. xanthina

QUEKETTIA

This is a genus of only a few species, from Venezuela, Brazil, and Argentina. Plants resemble Campanemias with fans of leaves and narrow tubular yellow-green flowers that can appear at any time of the year. Grow the plants in the sun and keep them moist all year. They do well on slabs or in fine-grade fir bark.

Q. *microscopica*
Q. *pygmaea*

RANGAERIS

Mainly from Uganda, Nigeria, and West Africa, these small orchids are valued for their lovely spurred white flowers. Leaves are narrow and flat—dark green. Flowers appear in mid-summer or in mid-winter. Plants like sun and heat; grow in small pots with fine-grade fir bark. Rangaeris are lovely but hard-to-find plants.

R. *brachyceras*
R. *musicola*

TRICHOCEROS

These fascinating orchids, known as Fly orchids, resemble the insect. Males are lured to the plant by what appears to be the female of the species. Plants have small pseudobulbs and stiff leaves. They need constant moisture and coolness (about 55°F.)—grow in a bright place. They are best cultivated on vertical slabs—plants branch out. The plant is a fine oddity.

T. *bergoldii*
T. *parviflorus*

GLOSSARY

Anther:	the sac containing pollen
Axil:	the upper angle between a stem or branch and a leaf
Back bulb:	old pseudobulb, usually without leaves
Bract:	a reduced leaflike organ protecting a flower stalk
Bulbous:	having the character of a bulb
Cultivar:	an individual plant in cultivation, including its vegetative propagations
Deciduous:	losing leaves at the end of the growing season
Division:	the means by which a single cultivar is divided into two or more plants
Epiphyte:	a plant that grows on another plant but is not a parasite, as it obtains nourishment from the air
Eye:	the bud of a growth
Family:	a group of related genera
Fragrans:	sweet-scented
Gene:	the unit of inheritance, located at a specific site on a chromosome
Genus:	a subdivision of a family consisting of one or more species that show similar characteristics and appear to have a common ancestry; adj., generic; pl., genera.
Habitat:	the locality in which a plant normally grows
Hybrid:	the offspring resulting from the cross between two different species or hybrids

Inflorescence: flowering, or the flowering part of a plant

Labellum: the lip of modified petal of an orchid flower (see lip)

Lead: a new vegetative growth

Lip: the labellum, usually quite distinct from the other two petals

Meristem: plant tissue consisting of actively growing and dividing cells

Monopodial: growing only from the apex of the plant

Node: a joint on a stem

Nomenclature: a system of naming

Parasite: a plant that lives on and derives part of all of its nourishment from another plant; adj., parasitic (cf. epiphyte)

Pendulous: hanging downward

Petal: one of the three inner segments of a flower, which is not modified to form the lip

Pistil: the female or seed-bearing organ of a flower consisting of the ovary, stigma, and style

Pollen: the fertilizing grains borne by the anther

Pollination: the transfer of pollen from the anther to the stigma

Pollinium: in orchids, a mass of pollen in the anthers; pl., pollinia

Pseudobulb: the thickened portion of a stem, but not a true bulb

Raceme: a simple inflorescence of stalked flowers

Rhizome: a root-bearing horizontal stem, which, in orchids, usually lies on or just beneath the surface of the ground

Rosette: a cluster of leaves arranged around a short stem

Sepal: one of the three outer segments of a flower

Species: a group of plants sharing one or more common characteristic(s) that make it distinct from any other group; adj., specific.

Spike: flower stem

Spur: hollow tubular extension of the lip

Sympodial: a form of growth in which each new shoot, arising from the rhizome of the previous growth, is a complete plant in itself; opposite of monopodial

Systemic: a pesticide that is absorbed by the plant and poisons the cells against pests.

Terete: circular in cross-section; sylindrical (cf. semiterete)

Terminal: at the end of the axis (cf. lateral)

Terrestrial: growing in or on the ground

Transpiration: the loss of water (by evaporation) from the plant tissue

Tuber: thickened, normally underground stem

Variety: a subdivision of a species; a group of plants that differs slightly from the main species type

Vegetative propagation: the increasing of a particular plant by division, or by meristem culture

Virus: an infectious agent that causes disease in living cells

SUPPLIERS OF PLANTS

Alberts and Merkel Bros., Inc.
P.O. Box 537
Boynton Beach, FL 33435

Black and Flory Ltd
Slough Bucks England

Charlesworth and Co., Ltd
Haywards Heath, Sussex, England

Creve Coeur Orchids
12 Graesner Acres
Creve Coeur, MO 63141

Dos Pueblos Orchid Co.
P.O. Box 158
Goleta, CA 93017

Fennell Orchid Co.
Homestead, FL 33030

Arthur Freed Orchids, Inc.
5731 S. Bonsall Dr.
Malibu, CA 90265

G. Ghose and Co., Orchids
Town-End, Darjeeling, West Bengal,
India

Hausermann's Orchids
(see Orchids by Hausermann)

Margaret Ilgenfritz
Ilgenfritz Orchids
P.S. Box 665
Monroe, MI 48161

Jones and Scully, Inc.
2200 N.W. 33rd Ave.
Miami, FL 33142

Oscar M. Kirsch
2869 Oahu Ave.
Honolulu, HI 97822

Wm. Kirsch Orchids, Ltd.
2630 Waiomao Rd.
Honolulu, HI 96816

Marcel Lecoufle
5 rue de Paris
Boissy-St. Leger, France

Lines Orchids
Taft Highway
Signal Mountain, TN 37377

Stuart Low Co.
Jarvisbrook (Crowborough)
Sussex, England

McBean's Cymbidium Orchids
Cooksbridge, Lewes, Sussex, England

Rod McLellan Co.
1450 El Camino Real
S. San Francisco, CA 94080

Oak Hill Gardens
P.O. Box 25, Rt. 2 Binnie Rd.
Dundee, IL 60118

Orchids by Hausermann
P.O. Box 363
Elmhurst, IL 60126

Orquideario Catarinense
P.O. Box 1
Corupa, Santa Catarina, Brazil

Joseph R. Redlinger, Orchids
9236 S.W. 57th Ave.
Miami, FL 33156

Rivermont Orchids
Signal Mountain, TN 37377

David Sander's Orchids Ltd
Selsfield, East Grinstead
Sussex, England

T. M. Sanders
12502 Prospect Ave.
Santa Ana, CA 92705

Santa Barbara Orchid Estate
1250 Orchid Dr.
Goleta, CA 93105

Walter Scheeren Orchids
Poestenkill, NY 12140

Sign of the Coon
Powderville, MT 59345

Earl J. Small Orchids, Inc.
6901 49th St.
Pinellas Park, FL 33565

Fred A Stewart, Inc.
1212 E. Las Tunas Dr.
San Gabriel, CA 91778

Tradewinds Orchids, Inc.
21800 S.W. 77th Ave.
Miami, FL 33156

Maurice Vacherot
31 rue de Valenton
Boissy-St. Leger, France

Wilkens Orchid Nursery
21905 S.W. 157 Ave.
Goulds, FL 33170

INDEX

Page numbers in **boldface** refer to illustrations.

Index · 194

Lankesterella, 183
L. ceracifolia, 183
L. orthnantha, 183
Leptotes, 126–27
L. bicolor, 23, 127
lighting:
  artificial, **29,** 48–50, **49**
  sun, 37, 43, 48, 59–60
  see also exposures; locations
locations:
  changing of, 41
  shade, 25, 26
  sunny, 25, 40
  window, 13, 27, 28, **29, 30**
Lycaste, 127–28
L. depeii, 23, 128

mail-order suppliers, 21
Malathion, 52, 54
Masdevallia, 19, 41, 128–36
M. bella, 26, 129
M. caudata, 26, 130
M. coccinea, 130, **131**
M. 'doris,' 131
M. horrida, 132
M. infracta, 132, **133**
M. peristeria, 133, **134**
M. schlimii, 135
M. schroederiana, 135
M. tovarensis, 26, 136
M. triangularis, 136
Maxillaria, 137–39, **137**
M. cobanensis, 138
M. tenuifolia, 138, **139**
M. variabilis, 139
mealybugs, 52, **53,** 54
Mexico, 24
Microcoelia, 140–41
M. exilis, 140
M. guyoniana, 141
Miltonia, 141–42

M. roezlii, 23
misting, 35, 48
mites, spider, 52, **53**
moon orchids, 20
mounting, 15, 27, 33–35
  on bark, **34**
  on racks, **32**
Mystacidium, 143
M. capense, 143

names:
  botanical, 19–20
  common, 20
Neolehmannia porpax, 112
New Guinea, 15
nicotine sulfate, 52, 54
nitrogen, 50
north light, orchids for, 26
Notylia, 183
N. bicolor, 183
N. xyphorius, 183
nurseries, 21, 22

offset division, **56,** 57
Oncidium, 14, **19,** 144–46
O. bahamense, 144
O. desertorum, 23, 145, **145**
O. leiboldii, 146
O. macropetalum, 23, 146
orchids:
  arboreal, **14,** 15–16, 17, 39
  beginner's list for, 23
  botanical vs. common names of, 19–20
  buying of, 21–22
  changing locations for, 41
  characteristics of, 16–17
  colors of, 17
  cost of, 22
  difficult, 181–85